PATENTS, TRADE MARKS AND DESIGNS IN INFORMATION WORK

Patents, trade marks and designs collectively called industrial property, are information sources of great value and importance. Research and development staff in both the academic and industrial worlds need access to industrial property information in order to ascertain what is already known and to implement property protection of their new discovery or product. The vast majority of what is published on the subject of industrial property is written from the standpoint of the legal profession and offers little practical help to student or practising information scientists and librarians. This book details the documentation in industrial property: how to create it, how to search for it and how the information is used — apart from its legal functions. Current developments in international law are reviewed and the book concludes with a look at other legislation which relates to industrial property.

Tamara S. Eisenschitz is a Lecturer in Information Science, City University, London

PATENTS, TRADE MARKS AND DESIGNS IN INFORMATION WORK

TAMARA S. EISENSCHITZ

CROOM HELM
London • New York • Sydney

© 1987 Tamara S. Eisenschitz
Croom Helm Ltd, Provident House, Burrell Row,
Beckenham, Kent, BR3 1AT
Croom Helm Australia, 44-50 Waterloo Road,
North Ryde, 2113, New South Wales

Published in the USA by
Croom Helm
in association with Methuen, Inc.
29 West 35th Street
New York, NY 10001

British Library Cataloguing in Publication Data

Eisenschitz, Tamara S.
    Patents, trade marks and designs in
    information work.
    1. Patent searching   2. Industrial property
    I. Title
    608   T210
    ISBN 0-7099-0958-6

Library of Congress Cataloging-in-Publication Data

Eisenschitz, Tamara S., 1950-
    Patents, trade marks and designs in information work.

    Bibliography: p.
    Includes index.
    1. Industrial property. 2. Industrial property —
Great Britain. 3. Patent searching. I. Title.
K1500.E4 1987   346.04′8   87-6776
ISBN 0-7099-0958-6   342.648

Printed and bound in Great Britain
by Billings & Sons Limited, Worcester.

CONTENTS

Acknowledgements

A number of people have helped me with both the style and content of this book. My greatest thanks are due to Dr Jeremy Phillips of the Intellectual Property Law Unit, QMC London, who helped edit the work and improve my English as well as making suggestions as to contents. He acted as a quality controller and this book is much improved as a result. Dr C Oppenheim and Mr H A van Asselt both read parts of the text and suggested small improvements of content and level of explanation. Also I wish to thank in a general way all the students on my courses at City University who have taught me how to put this subject across. Any errors or infelicities left in this work are, of course, my own responsibility. Despite all the good offices of my colleagues there are bound to be some. Lastly I must thank my various typists especially Tracy Levy who did so much to help with the word processing.

In the text, two front pages of British patents are included, those of 1302 268 and 2049 570A. There are also a few extracts from the UK patent classification. I thank the Controller of Her Majesty's Stationery Office for permission to publish these.

Preface

This book is intended as an introduction to industrial property for information workers and technical research workers. The text has grown out of a lecture course I give at the City University, Department of Information Science. It should serve as a source book for that course containing many intricate details that may be useful but for which there is not enough time on the course. By the same token it will be useful to students on information studies courses elsewhere. It will also serve the same purpose for scientists, technologists and managers who need to understand how to use this type of literature.

The introduction sets the scene and stresses the unity of concepts in this subject area. Then there are separate sections for the different types of law. The last section deals with EEC law and this emphasises unity again since the same principles apply to all the main types of industrial property.

The references in the bibliography are numbered indedpendently for each section and are listed in numerical order as they appear in the text. The index is fairly short because major items are highlighted by the contents table.

SECTION 1   INDUSTRIAL PROPERTY IN GENERAL

Chapter 1   Introduction

Patents, designs and trade marks are collectively known as **industrial property.** They confer valuable commercial rights enforceable under specific laws. The documentation associated with the claim or grant of these rights is an important body of information with both technical and commercial applications.

This book is designed to focus on the documentation, how to search for it and on how the information can be used other than in its legal capacity.

At its widest the field is known as **intellectual property** (1),

intellectual   industrial
property   =   property   + copyright

Copyright deals with the protection of literary, artistic, musical and dramatic works and their manifestations in print, recordings etc. We will not consider them in this book. But copyright also has an industrial component, it protects engineering drawings and mass produced items of artistic craftsmanship. Nevertheless we will refer to our field of interest as being primarily industrial property, and intellectual property will only be mentioned on the occasions when industrial property principles embrace copyright too. Reference to "designs" will include industrial copyright unless specifically excluded. The two are closely intertwined. Industrial property laws see to the **protection of creative**

ideas expressed in tangible form. An inventive concept must be reduced to a usable device or mechanism. A trade mark must be applied to a named product or service. A design must be applied to specific products like T-shirts or coffee cups or be the shape of a product as with a lampshade or a vase.

Intellectual property is protected separately in each country by its own laws, but there is also some regional and international protection available. In this book the UK situation is the main one to be considered, followed by that of the EEC and its various member states, and the worldwide international conventions. The systems employed in the USA are described in view of the industrial and trading importance of the USA. By our legal system of precedents and comparison of decided cases, UK law shares a common heritage with the USA and Commonwealth countries despite our joining the EEC and so reference to Commonwealth systems are made where necessary.

This volume is not intended for lawyers or other professionals who work habitually with industrial property. They rapidly gain familiarity with the minutiae of law and procedure, and most books on the subject go into vast detail on these topics. This text is intended for information scientists, and also for technical staff and managers who need to use the industrial property system for a range of technical and commercial purposes beyond the circular one of gaining and defending rights or probing those of others. I say "circular" because the system exists to administer these rights and the quid pro quo for the public of usable information is only valid when the material is used outside the cycle of obtaining, defending and infringing these rights. There are clear technical applications for patent information outside the cycle. The material in designs is similarly of some technical interest but also of a less specific aesthetic interest. Trade marks have a function in business information linking products and services to their producers. A contrast to intellectual property use is trade secrecy. Here there are no rights and also no information provision.

Although this book is concerned with technical and business information, a considerable knowledge of law and procedure is required as background for making use of the information.It is the difficulty of acquiring this knowledge relatively painlessly which ensures that industrial property matters remain an arcane backwater. They constitute a valuable resource, but lack of understanding by the engineers, scientists and craftsmen who generate it, by the management who largely overlook it and by the information and library professions who should be digesting and interpreting it, prevent effective exploitation of this commonly available material.

I shall attempt here to break down barriers in the way of exploitation.There are so many subdivisions that no segment is so long as to become confusing. Also there are summaries at convenient breathing spaces to clarify the main argument. There is a section for each of the main types of industrial property plus one on related legislation which encompasses existing and planned measures fulfilling a similar role to that of industrial property.There is also a section on EEC law. Since this affects all forms of industrial property in a similar way, it is logical to discuss them all together.

In this section a number of concepts are introduced which are common to all forms of industrial property. They will be discussed in detail in relevant later chapters, but their common aspects are brought together here. Some of the parts of this section will therefore need to be reconsidered after digesting the contents of the later ones.

Chapter 2   The Property Concept

English law divides into two main parts: criminal and civil(2).

Criminal Law
The criminal law mediates in disputes between an individual and the state. The punishment imposed is a generalised one such as imprisonment or the payment of a fine to the state. In part these reflect the attitude of public opinion as a whole or at least of the Government to a particular type of offence.
There is a small criminal component to industrial property offences which occurs mainly in the form of a distinct crime such as fraud. In criminal law, property is defined as something that can be stolen,ie taken permanently from its owner.But when information is taken, the owner is not thereby deprived of it.Therefore, to the extent to which industrial property consists of information, it cannot be stolen.Nevertheless one can frame offences using different legal concepts and in this way the criminal law does have a minor part to play in this area.These associated laws will be considered later in Section 5.

Civil Law
The main thrust of law and practice is directed towards the civil law which mediates in disputes between private individuals, businesses and other discrete enterprises. A familiar example of a civil dispute is one over a boundary between two tracts of land. The machinery of the law provides a fair, impartial procedure for the determination of rights. Each side should feel that its case has been fully considered even when the end result is

4

not the desired one. The state via its judges plays the arm's length role of referee and is never directly involved.

The concept of **property** in English civil law is wide ranging and quite complex. It covers land (real property) and movable possessions (personal property). Examples of different types of property are tabulated below.

real property		**personal property**	
tangible	**intangible**	**tangible**	**intangible**
land	rights of way	tables etc	stocks
buildings	restrictive	approx. all	shares
etc	covenants	"things" not	patents
	etc	fixed to the	etc
		ground	

Thus industrial property is intangible personal property. The property resides not in the tangible object given protection but in the right given to the owner to exploit the object and to prevent others from so doing.

Once the property concept has been accepted, industrial property has the same characteristics as all other forms of property:
    it can be sold (assigned),
    rented out to others (licensed)
    in exchange for rent (royalties),
    inherited via a will,
    mortgaged,
    counted as an asset in bankruptcy proceedings.

Thus in civil law the property concept is mainly an economic one (something one makes money from).

Let us now define the specific types of industrial property available in Britain. There are many variations between countries so that this is only an indication of possibilities.

(a) A **patent** gives a limited term of up to 20 years' monopoly for a new and useful invention. The owner has the exclusive right to make, use or sell products incorporating the invention. A particular subset of patentable material is that of rights over living things. Newly created micro organisms are patentable. Higher plants can be protected by plant varieties' rights legislation which are described in Section 5. There is no protection for higher animals (3).

(b) A **registered design** may be obtained for the overall appearance of a product or for a design printed on a product. The maximum term is 15 years. Many countries give 25 years protection and the 1985 white paper on intellectual property proposes that the UK term should also be 25 years (4).

(c) **Industrial copyright** often applies in parallel to registered designs. A design drawing may carry copyright as an artistic work. If it is realised in a three dimensional form or printed onto a product, the design as applied will be protected either by a registered design or by copyright. Either protection can apply and both will terminate together leaving only the pure drawing un-applied still protected as a work of art (5).
Craftworks in three dimensions without any drawings can have full copyright protection as **works of artistic craftsmanship.** This was designed to protect such works as Chippendale chairs.
Drawings for objects where appearance does not count (no eye appeal), and the objects themselves, are at present protected by full copyright as they are not eligible for design registration. This is inappropriate as being too long and too strong. The 1986 White Paper proposes a new **unregistered design right** to cover them. It would last for ten years only and protect against reproduction and sale (6).

(d) **Trade marks** give a product a brand identity. They connect the product to its manufacturer so that a customer knows exactly the source of his purchases. In this way a manufacturer can build up a reputation for the quality of his products. This protection lasts potentially for as long as the mark is used in relation to products. From October 1986 trade mark registration was extended to cover services as well as goods. For both goods and services it is common to have unregistered trade names, and customary use of these attracts common law protection under the designation of "passing off". This usage is much older and much more widespread than that of registered trade marks (7).

These are very brief definitions and they will be elaborated in the relevant sections. There is a common thread of protecting personal creative effort, the protection being bounded by the need to protect the perceived public interest.

Related Legislation
Some creative subject-matters fall within these areas of industrial property but not neatly into one category. They could be squeezed into one, spread between several or given a special protection for themselves. This last approach is called sui generis protection. **Computer programs** fall into this category: are they inventions to be patented or are they literary works to be copyrighted? **Technical drawings** are another example, the proposed ten years unregistered design right is a special sui generis protection.

Other subject-matter does not fit at all into the given categories despite the fact that similar problems of exploitation have arisen. Related legislation enacted and planned covers analogous rights such as control of the contents of **data** in various files both computerised and manual and the safekeeping of **information given in confidence.** For instance, an additional and complementary remedy for the deception practised in trade mark infringement is provided by the **Trade Descriptions Act.** There are a number of overlapping provisions between the two sets of legislation. An entire field of conflict revolves round the concept of **unfair trading practices** : that one should not be allowed to reap what others have sown. In Britain there is no such concept enshrined in a legal instrument. It has crept through the back door via sympathetic but strained interpretations of existing intellectual property laws. Some writers have suggested that these extensions need to be rethought. If a general code of trade ethics is required it should be incorporated into a specific Act rather than surreptitiously applied. Current trends in intellectual property can be understood most clearly in relation to unfair trading. The 1986 White Paper indicates the Government's acceptance that intellectual property is an instrument of trade policy.

Chapter 3   Multiple Protection

One of the reasons why industry greatly values the protection given by industrial property is that different components give protection to various facets of a product, the totality giving a far more secure protection than would appear from the separate consideration of each one. For instance, a rocking chair can be awarded a patent for mechanical improvements, a registered design for its styling and shape, and a trade mark for its brand name.

When we consider a product we can ask what modes of protection are available to it.This also shows us the many different angles from which a product can be attacked and pirated ensuring loss of revenue to its backers and ultimately higher prices to its consumers. The pirate's customers avoid paying the higher price, but the quality of goods they receive may well be lower than that of the genuine article.

Research in progress. A pharmaceutical compound could have patent protection for the compound and methods of making it. In Britain this lasts for up to twenty years from the date of application. But application is made very early in the life of the product so that more development work still needs to be done. Once the final product is devised, extensive safety testing is required before a licence to market is granted. So the patent really protects this long period of development. The time available for selling the product while it is protected is relatively short: say from five to ten years. This is why the pharmaceutical industry is always in the forefront of those demanding a longer patent lifetime. Outside the pharmaceutical industry the timing is not so tight. Unless a rival researcher is suspected, the patent application will be left as late as possible. Also there is much less testing to be done.

Brand loyalty. Even before a product is put on sale it can be given a brand name which is protected as a registered trade mark. With appropriate advertising brand loyalty can be created, so that when the patent protection is lost and other manufacturers sell the same product under different names, a hold will still be maintained on the market. Trade mark registration can be renewed indefinitely as long as the brand name is used. This relationship between trade marks and patents can be exploited for any product distinctive enough for a brand name to create loyalty. "Xerox" machines are a case in point. Xerox is the registered trade mark of the inventors of this type of photocopying machine. For many years as long as their main patents remained in force, one could obtain only Xerox brand photocopiers. Now there is strong competition from German and Japanese and other copiers, but the mark "Xerox" still retains its significance as an established type of machine.

Passing off. Apart from the formal protection given by a trade mark registration, the name and "get-up" of a product obtain protection from the common law of deception,that another trader should not "pass off" his goods or business as another's(8). There is no statute here, no Passing Off Act. The common law is the unwritten law of the people, of "natural justice" enshrined in the King's courts and passed on by recorded precedent cases rather than enshrined in codified laws. In this case natural justice says that no trader should take advantage of any reputation built up by another trader. This is clearly analogous to a trade mark right. The main difference is that the plaintiff, the trader who brings the action, has first to show that he does have a reputation in those goods, that the buying public associates his name with those goods. Only then can he accuse another of interfering with that association. If a registered trade mark is shown,the trader's reputation is assumed. Once a reputation is established a passing off action takes broadly the same course as a trade mark infringement action. The protected matter can be a name, a device or the get-up which can be the general shape and colouring of the product or its packaging or even the configuration and wording of the advertising slogans used to sell it. Examples will be given in the appropriate chapter.

As already mentioned, registered design and industrial copyright protection overlap. They protect the same attributes of a product and together would provide double protection. This being regarded as undesirable, the Acts lay down that when either one applies, the other is rendered inapplicable. Multiple protection of a product is permitted only when different attributes are being protected. It is the creativity of the owner rather than the product itself that is the focus of attention. This overlap occurs in Britain. In other countries the criteria of what deserves this type of protection varies considerably.

These are the main forms of protection, however there are others applying to specialised material. For instance, with computer programs much reliance is placed on user contracts to regulate reproduction of a program and distribution of the output resulting from their use.

Chapter 4   International Agreements

One of the most important characteristics of all industrial property is its potential for international exploitation which requires an international administration. Because trade in matter protected by industrial property has no geographical limitations, protection should ideally be available world wide.

In general, each country lays down its own procedures, therefore each country's legal system is different. They are, however, brought closer together and sometimes interconnected by a number of international conventions. These are effective because they are mainly administrative and take the substance of each national law as it is given. Some do set standards for each country to attain in its own way and form a basis for the increasing similarities between national systems. Most important countries are members of the conventions because they do not derogate from national sovereignty and yet ease international cooperation. In this way they are a positive example of international unity to be followed in other areas where possible.

The major part of international administration is carried out by one body:**WIPO, the World Intellectual Property Organisation.** WIPO is a UN agency based in Geneva where it has its own building and a permanent secretariat. It organises conferences and training sessions and administers conventions, holding all signatures, ratifications and amendments and providing meeting space and expertise for all the committees and other work associated with the conventions (9).

WIPO came into being in 1970 but is only the most recent embodiment of international cooperation. Its origins go back to 1883 when the **Paris convention** was adopted. This convention applies to industrial property in its widest sense and currently has 97 member states. This broad coverage makes the Paris convention still the most important in the field of industrial property. Soon afterwards in 1886 the **Berne convention** for the protection of literary and artistic works was also adopted. This regulates copyright protection and currently has 76 member states. Both conventions provided for an international secretariat to be established and the two were united in 1893. This joint bureau has functioned under various names. The predecessor of WIPO was called BIRPI, the acronym in French of"United International Bureaux for the Protection of Intellectual Property".

WIPO had 112 members all together as of January 1st 1986. It has accumulated quite a number of treaties and conventions elaborating protection in various specialised areas of intellectual property as well as the general conventions.

Apart from WIPO, there are other international organisations involved in one or more particular topics stemming from industrial property rights. For instance the **World Bank** is concerned with free trade and played a part in setting up **GATT** and **UNCTAD**. These have a bearing on international exploitation of industrial property focussing as they do on freedom of competition and on transfer of help for development from rich countries to poorer ones. UNCTAD has developed a **transfer of technology code** which is arguably more important than all the agreements on patent information because it concerns directly usable information on fully developed products. Industrial property does not function at this level of practicality at all. International agricultural organisations such as **FAO** are concerned with protection of **rights over varieties of plants** and also of animals. WIPO administers the existing convention on plants, **UPOV**. FAO and others input and channel thoughts and policies on how protection should further develop. There has been much concern about loss of genetic diversity and exploitation of third world peasant farmers.

Industrial Property and the EEC

The EEC is a body primarily devoted to the establishment of free competition among trading nations: free movement of workers, goods and services across frontiers. This sits ill with the concepts of industrial property, which allow for exclusive rights within national boundaries (10). The following is an example of a typical transaction. Two traders in country A and country B each derive their rights from the national IP laws of A and B respectively. They may be selling an identical product at different prices. If a third party buys at the lower price in A and imports the product into B, he can sell it there, undercutting the "legitimate" price in B. The IP laws of B would forbid such imports and resales as the third party has no authorisation to trade from the rights owner. Now the EEC Treaty comes in and asserts the primacy of free movement of goods. This is asserted by deciding that once goods have been sold anywhere in the EEC, their movement cannot be further regulated, national IP laws become inoperative.

The EEC Treaty does not abolish industrial property rights. It recognises the interest of an individual to have some control over the results of his creativity and labour. Also it recognises the value of such rights for the EEC as a whole in dealing with non-EEC countries.

The doctrine evolved by the EEC Commission and Court of Justice states that free movement of goods and services is central to the existence of the EEC and therefore takes priority over all other interests. Industrial property rights can be exercised but their scope will be limited so as not to interfere with free competition within the Community. This policy applies to copyright and by analogy to all intellectual property. Since the doctrine is transferrable from one property type to another, they all need to be examined together.

Origins of EEC policy and law

The EEC is a federation of independent states. In most areas of policy, the Council of Ministers retains the right of final decision. The Council consists of all appropriate Ministers seconded by their governments for the subject under discussion and is a Council of agriculture ministers or finance ministers or industry ministers or any other ministers. They will act in the national interest of their own country rather than in a specific EEC interest because they are accountable to their national electorates and parliaments. The specific EEC interest is articulated by the Commission, a full time civil service recruited from all the member states. They formulate policies but are normally subordinate to the Council of Ministers.

Uniquely, in the area of competition policy the Commission is sovereign. It formulates the policies and carries them out. It was recognised that in this area, the prime function of the EEC, national interests would tend to resist subordination despite it being in their best interests to be subordinate.Therefore competition policy is left entirely in the hands of the Commission.

The law is written down in the EEC Treaty. This Treaty is a combination of three treaties consolidated to bring about the unified EEC Treaty. There are in addition individual Acts of Parliament incorporating the Treaty into national laws upon accession. The articles of the Treaty are the only authority the Commission has to wield. If something is written in the Treaty it is legal. If not, then the activity has no right of existence but may nevertheless be carried on as an act of political will.

In accordance with the legal traditions of continental Europe, the Treaty provisions are broad statements of principle unlike the detailed statute law of the UK. Within their guidelines, the Commission has had considerable latitude in deciding the form of the laws to be followed. It issues them as regulations. The detailed interpretations of the Treaty and the regulations become law by being considered by the judges of the European Court of Justice (ECJ) in the light of individual cases brought before them. Judgments set out the reasoning used and these are enshrined as precedents in the law reports. These precedents are not rigidly adhered to but form guidelines and will be followed unless specific reasons for a contrary policy are accepted.

Cases will either be those brought against a firm by the Commission following a complaint and investigation, or they will be between two organisations. Those brought by the Commission are tried and decided by the ECJ itself. One organisation in dispute with another will bring its case before a national court.The national court can send a question to the ECJ which will give an authoritative statement of EEC law. Application of the law to the facts will then be carried out by the national court. Both ECJ judgments and statements of law are generally reported and form the basis of EEC case law.

To summarise, EEC law consists of the content of the Treaty interpreted in light of a considerable body of case law to fit the facts of a particular case.

Existence/exercise doctrine

Article 222 of the Treaty guarantees the existence of national property rights. Nothing in the Treaty is to prejudice national property laws and this should include rights over intellectual property. Despite this, the Commission feels that the unfettered exploitation of intellectual property rights would diminish the fundamental right of free movement of goods. Therefore property rights still **exist** but may only be **exercised** if this exercise does not conflict with the essential purposes of the Treaty.

Exhaustion of rights doctrine

Commercial rights flowing from intellectual property holdings are not limitless. They become exhausted once the proper nature of the right has been exercised. All further exercise oversteps what can legitimately be protected and must be stopped. This conclusion is the corollary of the existence/exercise doctrine.

A series of cases have determined that the legitimate rights consist of first entry into the market of goods handled under the rights and of suing for infringement anyone who puts the goods into the market without permission. Further handling of legally marketed goods is not protected. This covers imports of these goods into other countries plus restrictive agreements to prevent consumers having free access to otherwise legitimate competitors.

Intellectual property rights are treated as a branch of unfair competition legislation. The development of a consistent line of cases has been slow and involves a wide range of considerations other than the formal laws of patents, trade marks, designs and so on. Therefore this topic will be further dealt with at the end of the book, in Section 6, where the development of the doctrine through case law can be traced.

Chapter 5   Benefits of Industrial Property

The general public benefit from industrial property lies in dissemination of technical and commercial information. This shares ideas around industry, traders and researchers and stimulates further creativity. These benefits do nothing directly to assist those who actually obtain the rights. The various types of industrial property survive only because individual businessmen see advantages for themselves in obtaining protection for their property. What are the benefits that these exclusive rights confer? (11).

Patents

A patentee has exclusive rights to manufacture a protected product or use a protected process. He can do this in one country and then import it into another. This allows for breathing space without competition during which the market can be secured and the quality and value of the invention demonstrated.

If a patentee cannot carry out all phases of an invention himself, then he can license others to do so. If the invention is capable of commercial exploitation, this brings in an income without the need to take risks. If an invention is to be exploited in more than one country, then one or more licensees will be needed to control the enterprise in the different countries due to sheer size.

Most inventions are made nowadays by employees and any resulting patents belong to their employers, usually companies. Company patenting policy is very variable, but some of the most valuable uses of patents are as commercial bargaining counters with rival firms in the same technology. One can set a value on a patent and either sell it outright or issue a licence. A slight variation on this is for a group of companies to get together and create a patent pool: all research and development is shared and members can use any patent freely. Unfortunately, R & D agreements which break down are a fruitful source of litigation, often worldwide and prolonged. An example of this was the agreement between Beechams and Bristol-Myers, both large pharmaceutical companies, to work together on developing synthetic penicillins. A series of cases have been fought in various countries over patents covering the Amoxycillin group and in particular the Ampicillin patent.

Trade Marks

The protection here is given to the brand name of goods or services and for associated designs or packaging. These may also denote quality of a product by giving their origin, either a manufacturer or sometimes a reputable trader who endorses the produce of certain manufacturers. This is common among chain stores such as Marks and Spencer with the "St Michael" label. Registration of trade marks in the UK became available for services as well as for goods only in late 1986, many years behind most other countries.

The sale or licensing of registered trade marks is more complicated than that of patents because the entire business goodwill is bound up with the mark. The need not to confuse the purchasing public is paramount, and the mark and its origin must be kept closely associated.

If a mark or design or get-up is not registered but is distinctive of a certain manufacturer's goods, the common law of passing off gives virtually the same protection except that distinctiveness must first be proved which is by no means easy. Trade mark registration obviates that step but, as will be described later, is not always permissible even when desired.

18

Designs

Registered designs protect the eye appeal of an object. As with patents they allow a short time for production to get under way before competition is allowed in. It applies to such items as the shapes of vases and lamps, to the pictures on the sides of coffee cups, to the shapes of furniture and to the shapes of costume jewellery. It also applies to designs on wallpaper and fabrics.

Where design registration is not allowed, for instance in respect of technical drawings of machinery, such drawings are protected by copyright. The machinery made from these drawings is also protected but indirectly as a realisation of the drawings. In this way car manufacturers have obtained a considerable income from licences to spare parts manufacturers that enable them to make those parts. Designs are so constrained by the space available within the given whole, that it is usually impossible to make such parts differently from the manufacturers' specifications. Therefore the parts come under the protection of copyright law. This protection is very controversial and in the specific case of spare parts has been removed by the recent House of Lords ruling of **British Leyland v Armstrong.**

The benefit available here for designers is limited protection from competition in objects of identical or very similar appearance and for virtually unlimited protection from competition for manufacturing plans in cases where the designs are utilitarian and have no aesthetic appeal. Protection which lasts for the life of the designer plus fifty years is far longer than the lifetime of most functioning machinery with very few exceptions, so that this protection is unlimited for all practical purposes. It is also a protection unique to the UK. Under current proposals it will be replaced by the ten year unregistered design right.

In the appropriate chapters these forms of protection will be elaborated with detailed examples. In this section we see that they are all essentially similar. It is very easy to become bogged down in the technicalities of one form of protection and to forget that the strength of industrial property laws lies in the multifaceted web of protection they weave around a product.

Summary

1. Industrial property is a form of intangible personal property. It can be traded for money, mortgaged, inherited or rented out just as any other item of property.

2. Industrial property consists broadly of patents, trade marks and registered designs and industrial copyright. Related matters of know-how, plant variety rights, confidential information and unfair trade practices need also to be included to provide a rounded picture. A product can be protected in different aspects by one or more of the forms of industrial property. Protection is also available via a number of less well defined related measures such as passing off, control of know-how or protection of confidential information.

3. Because trade is potentially worldwide, protection in different countries needs to be coordinated. To do this there are a number of international conventions, administered mainly by WIPO which help link the provisions of national laws. The most important convention is the Paris Convention for the Protection of Industrial Property, 1883.

4. Policy on industrial property in the EEC is dictated by the pre-eminence of the doctrine of free movement of goods. Property rights are allowed to exist but the proper nature of these rights has to be defined. A right may be exercised only to the extent of its "essential nature". Any wider attempt to exercise rights serves more to hamper competition than to relate to the property and such rights are not allowed to be enforced within the EEC.

Benefits of Industrial Property

5.   Industrial property is only obtained where an
     individual industrialist can see benefit in
     it for himself. Therefore the public benefits
     which accrue from such property, in
     particular the information aspects, are
     limited and balanced by benefits to the
     industries which use them.

SECTION 2   PATENTS

Chapter 1   Introduction

The granted patent forms a bargain or contract between a government and an inventor.

The **inventor** makes a new and useful invention and deposits in a public place a description of the invention written in sufficient detail for a skilled man to carry it out. This description must be written in such a way to be clear to a man skilled in the relevant "art", a general term to describe a body of technical knowledge.

The **government** gives a monopoly for a fixed number of years, this period being an upper limit.The monopoly confers upon the patentee the exclusive right to make, use or sell the invention, to import it or to authorise others to do these things. In Britain the statutory maximum period was first 14, then 16 and now 20 years, these being the normal maximum periods allowed in actively patenting countries.

From this definition of a patent it is clear that they are of great importance as information sources. The requirement to deposit an account of an invention means that in a patent library there will repose detailed descriptions of all types of technology in all their stages of development. Thus the progress of a particular art and its current state can be charted. Problems to be solved can be pinpointed and competing firms and active inventors identified. This information is used for both technical and commercial purposes and frequently for a combination of the two.

The requirement that descriptions need to be comprehensible to those skilled in the art does mean that only the facts immediately surrounding a problem and its solution are given. Someone wishing to find out about an unfamiliar art would need first to find a general description of the technology elsewhere. Only when a completely new technology, such as the hovercraft or the electronic computer, is introduced, are the descriptions complete for a wider range of readers. This restriction does reduce the general usefulness of patent specifications but it is necessary as otherwise each specification would require a thick tome, most of which would consist of a lengthy recital of existing knowledge.

Chapter 2   Brief History

Patent systems were set up and encouraged by
various governments to encourage growth in the use
of technology and development of improved
technologies (1). Before formal laws were passed
to control patents for inventions, there were in
England "letters patent", open letters from the
King, granted to foreign craftsmen to allow them
to settle in this country and practise their
trade, provided they taught apprentices all their
skills. One of the earliest was given in 1331 to a
Flemish weaver. A patent could also be granted to
an individual for a specific purpose. Thus in 1449
Thomas Utynam was granted a patent for the
manufacture and supply of stained glass for the
windows of Eton College chapel. Documents relating
to these very early letters patent are to be found
in the official papers in the Public Records
Office at Kew in London.

Similar provisions for attracting craftsmen were
enacted in other European countries. Probably the
earliest law concerning protection of inventions
was that passed in the City State of Venice in
1474. This allowed an inventor monopoly rights to
exploit his product so that the ease of trading
with no competition for his particular improvement
would encourage him to make further inventions.
Under this law Galileo was granted a patent in
1594 for a device for raising water and irrigating
the land.

In Britain, the Crown's privilege of granting
monopolies became abused and in 1624 the **Statute
of Monopolies** was passed(2). This outlawed all
monopolies except in respect of inventions.
Patents were to be granted to "the true and first

inventor" for "the sole working or making of any manner of new manufacture within the realm". This was a landmark Act but has no connection with modern practices.In particular it required by way of documentation of the invention, only a statement of the approximate topic covered. The result was that at this time only the patent grant was recorded, no details of an invention were published.

As technology became more complex, applicants began voluntarily to provide a description of their inventions so as to make it clear what protection had been awarded. This prevented other applicants from laying claim to the same invention. Some of the early accounts were pretty scanty and it was only in the mid 1700's that provision of a **written description** became the norm. This document was expected to contain a useful amount of detail. The Arkwright patent for spinning machines was ruled invalid in 1785 because insufficient detail was given about how to implement the invention(3). This was the first time an information requirement for the specification was laid down and was thus an important step in the development of patents as an information source. It has been suggested that in Britain deposit of a document in conjunction with a patent application was made compulsory in analogy with the requirement to deposit a work when obtaining copyright protection.Even then the descriptions were not published, merely inscribed on the King's rolls.

The patent system in Britain in this period was a confusing mess. Dickens helped lead a campaign for its reform and in 1852 a single comprehensive law, the **Patent Law Amendment Act** was passed(4). This established a Patent Office for the entire UK and its first head was Bennett Woodcroft. He arranged for all subsequent patent specifications to be printed and also had such earlier ones as could be obtained from the Rolls copied and printed. These early specifications were given numbers 1 (published in 1617) to 14 359 (published in 1852).

Under the 1852 Act, patents were granted with a mere formalities check. This involved checking that a specification contained all relevant detail such as a title, inventor and at least one claim. The technical content was not checked. It was the responsibility of each inventor to check that their work was original. To this end Bennett Woodcroft established the Patent Office library holding British and foreign specifications and other technical literature. He had British patent specifications and their associated searching aids distributed to technical libraries all over the country with the proviso that they were made freely accessible to the public. He also helped institute the science museum to hold working models of previous inventions as an inspiration for others. A patent classification by subject and a number of indexes were established for the British patents to help the public search the specifications.

Examination for novelty in the British Patent Office only started in 1902. This gave more rigour to the granting of patents and led to ever more detailed classification to aid the examiners in their searches.

Patent Acts from then on retained the same basic pattern. There was a comprehensive statute in 1907 and also important amendments in 1932 and then the last "old" statute in 1949. They were all based on the Statute of Monopolies' definition of an invention as "any manner of new manufacture within the realm".

The **present Patent Act** is that of **1977** and its provisions are rather a break with tradition. A new system of examination with modified criteria was introduced and definitions of what is patentable were spelled out with examples(5).

Parallel to this British development, many other major countries acquired patent systems and regional and international agreements have been signed.

Apart from co-operation in the interests of perpetuating the patent system itself, there has been a lot of effort and investment in patent information systems now that it has become accepted that valuable information is held in these (at first glance) purely legal documents. The main manifestation of information contained in an application or in a granted patent is its specification, which we will now explore in more detail.

Chapter 3   The Patent Specification

Other than where specifically mentioned, the specifications and procedures of the Patents Act 1977 will be described. Two specifications are published in conjunction with a PA77 grant. The one labelled "A" is that submitted with the application. The one labelled "B" is published simultaneously with the grant of the patent. It defines the protection that is actually granted. The A specification is usually the more detailed one if there are differences, and is therefore the one used by information seekers. The precise content of the specification is laid down in the regulations issued alongside PA77 (6).

A specification can be divided into three parts:

3.1 the front page,
3.2 the body of the specification, and
3.3 the claims.

3.1 The Front Page
The front page carries a title, an abstract, a drawing (where one is appropriate) and a great deal of additional information added by the Patent Office before publication. See the example given in the accompanying Figure.

The **title** is intended to give the general area of the invention. The title of the given example : "Liquid transport and delivery" is not a misdescription but neither is it particularly informative. Often a title is utterly vague, such as "Chemical compound" or "Improvements in or relating to vehicles". In general, titles are useless as sources of information. They are headings and cannot stand alone.

The **abstract** does stand alone. It is written by the applicant and must contain a concise summary of the technical field, the problem and its solution. Principal uses and, where applicable, the most suitable form of the invention are to be mentioned. It is intended to give sufficient information about the invention and about its applications to serve as a substitute for the specification for a casual enquirer. The information needs to be well enough organised to indicate reliably to a searcher whether or not he needs to consult the full specification.

Both the title and the abstract may be rewritten by the patent examiner if he is not satisfied with them. There is no appeal so that if the examiner has misinterpreted the main point of an invention, provided this does not affect the claims it is virtually impossible to have them changed back. This happens surprisingly often. Note that the private company Derwent Publications rewrites all titles and abstracts to make them as useful as possible to industrial searchers of their printed and online services. These services are described in 8.2.

Other front page information

Document numbers. The application is given an application number on reception at the patent office. This number is of the type 8712345. The first two digits give the year and other five a running sequential application number which is reset at 00001 at the beginning of each year. When the application is published, it is given a document number in the 2 million series followed by an "A". If granted, the patent number is the same document number followed by a "B".

Inventor's and applicant's names. All inventors are entitled to be acknowledged on the front page. Usually the applicant's name is different, the main reason being that most inventions are made in the course of employment and the applicant will be the employer of the inventor. Applicants can be legal or natural persons, a legal person being a firm or other entity. An applicant other than the inventor must fill in a form stating his title to the patent. This must also be done by inventors who apply but leave other inventors out. This information and any other paperwork connected with

(12) **UK Patent Application** (19) **GB** (11) **2 049 570** **A**

(21) Application No 8013383
(22) Date of filing 23 Apr 1980
(30) Priority data
(31) 48939
(32) 4 May 1979
(33) Italy (IT)
(43) Application published
31 Dec 1980
(51) INT CL³
B60P 3/22 1/64
(52) Domestic classification
B7B 328 349 WA
(56) Documents cited
GB 1520213
GB 1468665
GB 1314587
US 3702661A
(58) Field of search
B7B
B7L
B8P
(71) Applicants
**Officine Romanazzi
S.p.A.,
1072 Via Tiburtina, 00156
Rome, Italy**

(72) Inventor
Paolo Romanazzi
(74) Agents
W. H. Beck, Greener & Co.

(54) **Liquid transport and delivery**

(57) An engine 1 tows one or more container tanks 3 arranged on a semi-trailer 2 in removable manner. At least one of the tanks 3 incorporates measuring and delivery plant 7.

Each tank 3 is situated inside a robust protective frame 4 which has the external dimensions of a standard container.

All the various container tanks can be operated and stacked in conventional fashion and they can be interconnected by means of flexible piping so as to constitute a single tank served by the plant carried by one of them.

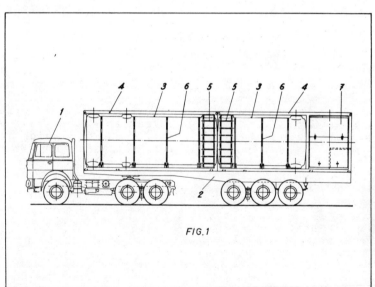

FIG.1

GB 2 049 570 A

the application is held in a file at the Patent Office. Files are opened to the public at the same time as the specification is published.

When the patent is granted, the applicant becomes the proprietor and patentee. In the USA, an owner of a patent is called the "assignee" because US patents can only be granted to inventors who may then assign the rights. This word is sometimes used in Britain as well. It tends to be used by large international information services which expect a large proportion of their users to be American.

In Comecon countries citizens are awarded inventors' certificates rather than patents. With these one cannot rely on a name search to be straightforward. The system of reward allows many names to be included on these certificates, only one or two of which will be those of the inventors. Many systems will enter only the first few names in their indexes and the inventor may well be missed out.

Dates. The dates on which the application is filed at the British Patent Office, and when it is published, are given. The date of grant and the simultaneous second publication is given on the B specification.

Priority data. If on a world wide view, the British application is the first one made for that invention, then this application establishes the priority date. This date is the date on which the inventor declares that he knows what is described in the application. He establishes his "priority" of knowledge on that date. If it is an application made under the International (Paris) Convention then the priority was established elsewhere in the country of first application. Thus the "priority data" are the country, application number and date of the original application. The priority date is the reference date for questions of novelty and inventive step. These will be discussed in the next chapter.

Domestic classification is the subject matter classification given to the invention by an examiner using the British patent classification (BPC). The examiners' search files and the searching aids available to the public are arranged by the BPC. Additional material put in the examiners' files, such as foreign patents and journal articles, are also classified by the BPC. These are not available to the public.

Int Cl is the international patent classification (IPC). The edition used is given as a raised suffix. Membership of the IPC Union (administered by WIPO) obliges each member state to print IPC symbols on all published patent documents. Many countries use only the IPC for their classification and searching, and this was indeed the intention of the founding members of the IPC treaty. However, as the BPC is a highly developed classification and has the advantage of being totally under the control of the examiners, the British Patent Office still keeps it as the primary classification scheme for UK patents. For the same reasons the Americans keep their own classification too. See Chapter 2.7 for details of these patent classifications.

Documents cited are documents the examiner has found which seem to have a bearing on the novelty or inventiveness of the present application. These documents will be mainly British patents, as it is only since the 1977 Act came into force that the examiners were required to search anything other than their own patents.

These documents can sometimes be very relevant. There could be a direct anticipation of the invention so that the details of the invention are given in the same or another context. The degree of novelty is determined by matching each item featured in the claims with an item in the cited document. Alternatively, there could be illustrations of different attempts to solve the problem tackled by the invention; this would indicate just how much of an inventive step the invention under consideration really was. Again, the cited documents could be merely providing background on the art for the examiner's benefit and have no direct relevance to the invention at all. The British search report gives no indication of the relevance of each document. As we will see later, European patents have their search report at the back. Each document is labelled with a code which indicates its relevance as background or to a particular claim.

Agents are the patent agents who drafted the application. Any applicant is entitled to write his own specification and steer it through all the stages of processing to grant. No one is entitled to do this for him for money except a registered patent agent or a solicitor. Patent agents serve a long apprenticeship, learning by doing in a patent agent's office. Their main job is to write a specification from the description provided by an inventor and take it through all stages of processing to grant. They can represent their clients in actions before or after grant in front of the Patent Office Comptroller, but must brief counsel if a case goes to the High Court. Thus they advise on patent related legal actions and also on licensing agreements. Many patent agents will also give advice on trade mark and copyright and design matters. In short their functions are very similar to those of solicitors but in a rather specialised area. The current White Paper on intellectual property proposes to expand the patent agent's role in litigation. Many actions which now go to the High Court would be confined to the Patent Office in order to save costs and time. The Board of Trade is also investigating the whole topic of patent agent's training and whether it would be desirable to allow professionals with different training to become involved in this work and provide some competition.

Most industrial applicants will employ a patent agent because if the patent turns out to be profitable, only a well written specification will stand up to the probing of competitors. This can be exceedingly hostile and destructive as they will try anything to gain a slice of the profits for themselves.

Foreign patents applied for under the Convention will almost certainly include an agent's name because all applications need a British address for service, to receive queries and demands for fees, and to serve as a general contact point for the Patent Office.

Most practising patent agents belong to the Chartered Institute of Patent Agents, CIPA, their professional body. CIPA encourages all agents to be members but strictly its only duty is to compile a register. Every year CIPA publishes this register of names and addresses. If an industrialist reads a patent specification and wants more details or would like to negotiate a licence, he can always look up the address of the patent agent in the CIPA register and get in touch. If an inventor needs a patent agent and no colleague can recommend one, then the register provides one way to find one. Agents are not currently allowed to advertise and organisations are not allowed to recommend one although a chamber of commerce or public reference library could hand out a list of local practices. On the other hand, there is nothing to stop patent agents being listed in the Yellow Pages.

INID numbers. All the entries on the front page have numbers in brackets on their left hand sides as in "(56) Document cited". See Figure 1 for the overall appearance of these numbers. They are the so called INID numbers. They were introduced in a programme of overall standardisation of content and layout of front pages in order to help with automatic processing of front page information. If number 56 means "document cited" on any patent in any language, then this is an easy retrieval marker for an automated system whether it involves punched cards or computers. The numbers are also good markers for picking out important items printed in an unfamiliar language.

The INID numbers were devised by ICIREPAT, the International Committee for Information Retrieval by Examining Patent Offices. Their aim is to improve information retrieval and the standardisation programme has been very successful. ICIREPAT has been responsible not only for the numbers, but also for standardising the layout and content of front pages of patents in WIPO affiliated countries. Older patents of most countries are not as informative on their front pages.ICIREPAT has been absorbed into the work of WIPO and its separate identity and name dropped.The actual acronym INID stands for "ICIREPAT Numbers for the Identification of Bibliographic Data".

The British Patent Office issues a free leaflet; "ICIREPAT codes and guidelines". This lists all the INID codes plus other details.Codes for major countries are also listed in the two Patent Office leaflets which outline the patent system and how to carry out a patent search (7).

3.2 The Body of the Specification

Here the invention is set into context and described in detail with examples.

First there is an **introduction** which states briefly what constitutes the invention with some indication of the prior art and the nature of the problem. The prior art is the sum of relevant foregoing knowledge with which the inventor works. There is no requirement in the Act for a comprehensive statement of the prior art, so this tends to be brief. The problem is that fresh prior art, found during the lifetime of the patent, may affect the interpretation of the invention, its significance and consequentially the validity of the patent. Prior art for an invention is defined as all knowledge before the priority date of the patent. When an invention is successful, competitors will comb the literature of the world looking for references to anything remotely similar and it is usually quite impossible to predict what might be found. One might expect this to be the job of the Patent Office, but, in the United Kingdom examiners undertake a restricted search only.They always leave open the possibility of further finds by third parties and rely upon parties with a vested interest to search more thoroughly. The possibility of unexpected challenges causes patentees to be careful not to state the reasoning which lead to their inventions too explicitly.

The statement of the problem being solved is also not in any way prescribed. If the inventor had in mind a definite and clear problem and set out to solve it, then the problem will probably be stated. But if the inventor had had a good idea just from his general knowledge then he will not try to set this out in problem and answer form if this was not how it was perceived in the first place. This flexibility is in contrast to the European Patent Office where a problem and solution approach is strongly favoured even if not strictly required.

The second stage is the **specific description** where the invention is described in detail. The invention may be a product or a process and the nature of the description will obviously vary depending on the field of technology involved. The description will first be as general as possible so as to take in all possibilities; it will then be elaborated by **examples**. These are called "preferred embodiments". Specific materials will be singled out as well as specific operating parameters such as a particular value out of a range of temperatures or angles. Often drawings are provided to clarify the explanations. Where alternatives are possible a number of examples may be given which will be sufficient to illustrate the entire range actually constructed by the inventor. It is not wise to make up examples which have not been tried out, because, if the invention does not work as described, its failure to do so might invalidate the patent.

All essential details have to be included or else an expert would not be able to reproduce the invention. On the other hand many essential details can be obscured by giving only ranges of values and possible substances. The best method of doing something has to be given if it is known but does not need to be singled out. A big problem is that it is only by trying the invention out that one can find whether the instructions are adequate. The examiners cannot do this and cannot therefore exercise really adequate control over the way the specifications are written.

A family of patents arises from applications for protection in a number of countries. The resulting texts interpreting the invention may well not look alike as requirements for a specification differ from country to country.For instance in West Germany and many other European states, it is normal for the prior art and description of the invention to be set out strictly in question and answer form. In the USA all prior art must be revealed and made available to the examiners. However, this need not appear in the specification as prior art as it can be revealed on a form to be kept in the Patent Office file. This latter requirement goes against the normal revelatory purpose of the patent system and seems surprising in a country which prizes openness and has much stricter rules than the UK on clarity of writing in patent specifications. J.Pinhey found that US claims are generally of narrower scope than British ones when she compared family members in the field of crystallography (8).

Returning to the British system, the description

must indicate that an advance, an inventive step, has been made but there are few explicit requirements. The body of the specification has to set out the invention in such a manner as to satisfy the requirement of disclosure to the public. This fictitious body of people is not the general public but is composed of experts in the art who know everything but are incapable of undertaking inventive activities themselves. The description is supposed to be written in clear and straightforward language, must not be misleading and must be consistent with the claims.

3.3 The Claims

This is a separate part of the specification and there will be a heading which reads "Claims" or "What I (we) claim is". The claims then follow in a numbered list.

The claims start very broadly and then get successively narrower with sometimes a second sequence of broad to narrow to illustrate a subsidiary feature of the invention. An inventor is not allowed to claim more than one invention in one patent but, if a pharmaceutical compound is claimed, then the capsules or tablets in which it is delivered are acceptable as secondary features of the invention and will have their own broad and narrow sequence of claims. Thus a patent can have quite a number of claims. The number of claims in the granted patent can be an indication of its strength. If only a few narrow claims are present, then the inventive area "staked out" is a narrow one. Broad claims implying wide protection indicate a much more substantial invention, although it is only when the claims have survived a challenge in court that they can be said to be truly valid.

The claims define the invention; they define the legal monopoly to be enjoyed by the patentee, although they must be interpreted in the light of the rest of the contents of the specification. The inventor wishes to obtain the widest possible protection for what is new and therefore must be careful not to include details in the description which would limit the scope of protection unnecessarily.

For the main claim, the widest one, only

absolutely essential components are included. Thus in a specification dealing with window frame lintels, before speaking of "perpendicular struts" one must ask if they really need to be at right angles and if not how far they can deviate from the vertical. If a working embodiment could be built without the struts at all, then they should be left out of the main claim.

In the second and subsequent claims, additional details are included, such as that vertical struts could be used and what materials they could be made from. The final claim is usually an "omnibus claim" : the invention as portrayed in the examples and drawings of the specification. In some countries omnibus claims are discouraged. It is apparent that the claims range from a very generalised statement down to specific embodiments in graduated steps. The wording of claims is crucial to their later usefulness and this is the particular skill of a patent agent. If one claim is challenged either by an examiner or later on in an infringement/revocation hearing it is possible that one or more of the others will survive and keep the patent or application in being. This is the reason for having many claims.

As an example of the critical importance of single words consider the Black and Decker "Workmate" (TM). This is a highly successful invention, it consists of two planks of wood which can be moved independently at either end to form a vice, and is otherwise a workbench for DIY enthusiasts. An accused infringer presented as prior art a book binding press which consisted of separately moving planks of wood between which a book would be held. The claims for the "Workmate" covered this press perfectly. Only one word did not fit and that was "workbench".The surface of the press was certainly not a workbench and because of this one word the "Workmate" patent was able to remain in force (9).

The specification as a whole must not be misleading or contain any false statements. During the twelve month convention period, a new specification can be introduced claiming priority from the previous one if amendments are to be made.Any new matter would then have the date of amendment as priority date.This is the reason why some patents have more than one priority date.

The Patent Specification

After twelve months, amendments are difficult as new matter may not be introduced. After publication, errors can only be corrected if the need for correction is obvious and the examiner gives leave.

Chapter 4   The Patent Grant

Throughout the world there are four basic patent systems in use. These are

1. Deferred examination-based;
2. Traditional;
3. Comecon;
4. Registration-based.

Because of variations of detail within these systems, it could be argued that there are more than four. But division into four seems to cover the main features and is sufficient for our purposes. When dealing with the patent system of any one country, its law needs to be understood in detail. For a first brief appreciation there exist compilations summarising the laws of many countries. The best, which are loose leaf, are frequently updated. Each sheet should have its printing date shown on it so that there can be no doubt as to currency. A good example is "Patents Throughout the World" published by Trade Activities Inc, New York.

4.1 Deferred Examination
The UK patent system is a deferred examination system and will now be described in detail. It is covered by the Patents Act 1977 which will subsequently be referred to as PA77.

4.1.1 The UK patent system
The deferred examination system is a new one for British patents, a break from the past. The previous Patents Act of 1949 was of the traditional variety, based on a pattern which was developed continuously from the Statute of Monopolies onwards. Differences between the 1949

and 1977 Acts will be pointed out as appropriate. The structure of the present Act is based on the recommendations of the Banks committee which produced a report based on submissions and on their analysis of the possibilities for reform (10).

What is patentable?

Three criteria of patentability are listed in PA77 Section 1(1).This is followed by a specific list of non-patentable subject matter in Section 1(2). The three general criteria are

> novelty
> inventive step, and
> industrial applicability.

Novelty and inventive step are judged in relation to the prior art. This is all material described in the literature. For patenting purposes, literature is material recorded in any form whatsoever: print, microforms, videotapes, photographs and so on. This material needs to be available to the public. If it is kept entirely in confidence, then it is not part of the prior art. The literature upon which the prior art is based needs to be defined with respect to time, countries, languages and availability. The definition is different when intended for novelty or for inventive step. It is also likely to be different when dealing with other countries.

Novelty

The invention must be new, which means that it must have been neither described in the prior art nor used publicly anywhere in the world at any time before the priority date of the patent. We will label these for reference as no prior publications and no prior user respectively.The requirement of worldwide or "absolute" novelty is in contrast to that of "local" novelty confined to the country in question. Local novelty is the system that was in force in Britain up to and including the 1949 Act and is in force in quite a number of middle range and small countries to this day. An exact reproduction of the invention in print or in use is required for an allegation of lack of novelty to succeed. However, a description which matches a set of claims can come from a different artifact. We have seen this in 3.3 with the comparison between the "Workmate" DIY worktop and a book binding press. If the Workmate were just a bigger book binding press, there would be no inventive merit in its new use. Being a workbench is its essential characteristic and the art of obtaining a patent is to identify such defining components.

No prior publications is the requirement concerning the published coverage. The prior art for this purpose is taken to be all literature published up to the priority date. This includes patents previously applied for but not yet published because the eighteen months period between the priority date and publication date has not elapsed. A subsequent applicant will not know about them until the eighteen months are up. It may seem to be unfair to include these applications but the philosophy is that the information already exists and will soon become available (whether or not a patent is granted). The existence of the first specification cannot be ignored, even though it is at present unpublished, when considering the benefit which the second applicant claims to confer on the world at large. If this benefit is sufficiently reduced, the state cannot justify the grant of a monopoly concession. There are special arrangements in the Act for innocent users who start to develop an invention for which an unpublished patent application exists. Such users may or may not also have applied for a patent for the same invention. The eventual patentee cannot stop them doing what they had prepared to do before they found out about the previous patent, but they cannot expand or develop further without coming to terms with the patentee.

Apart from earlier patents from all countries, the prior art consists of all forms of technical communication such as journal articles, conference proceedings, oral disclosures at scientific meetings, audio tapes, video tapes, microfilm and theses. Ph.D. theses in chemistry and engineering are often restricted to a small number of users for a few years after their completion in case any of the material is patentable. It is normal for theses to be held in the library of the university or other institution to which they were submitted and they are often held on closed access. However, if people can see the theses as of right, by asking for them at the library counter, they are regarded as having been published. The information they contain becomes part of the state of the art.

The question is not how many people are allowed to see a document but rather under what conditions of secrecy may the document be consulted. Publication takes place if even one individual is free to make any use he pleases of a document's contents with no obligation of confidence. In **Monsanto Company's (Brignac's) Application,**(1971), prior publication took place via an internal company bulletin of which forty copies were given to salesmen to distribute to possible customers (11). However, in **van der Lely v Bamfords,**(1963) (12), an engineer saw photographs of equipment without any explanations of function. Here expert advice was needed on how much technical knowledge an engineer could have gleaned from the photos and whether this was enough to guarantee production of the same product. It was held that the photograph was clear enough to reveal the inventive components in detail. Therefore the patent was anticipated and duly revoked.

No prior user is the requirement covering demonstrations and market trials. None must be carried out in public before the priority date. Experiments in secret are frequently conducted as part of developing an invention and, because they are secret do not count against novelty. Public demonstrations even to small groups and experiments in public places where they could be observed will invalidate an application. The same principle applies to individual visitors to the research laboratory where the apparatus is housed. As with prior publication the paramount consideration is that of secrecy. A demonstration to a select few is not public, providing the audience has been informed of the obligation of confidence.

This rule constitutes one reason why casual visitors to research laboratories should be, and usually are kept away from areas where inventive work is carried out. If visitors are allowed in they can take note of devices and processes without giving an undertaking as to confidence and this would count as giving a public demonstration. Requiring all visitors to sign a confidentiality form at the outset does not solve the problem as it has been held that if too many people are

admitted to a confidential relationship, the
essential characteristic of confidentiality is
lost. In the case of **Fomento v Mentmore**,(1956)
(13), three newly developed pens were given away
as presents and the recipients were held to be
prior users conducting a market trial of the
product.

**What does the examiner's novelty search consist
of?**
Under the Patents Act 1949, novelty was local,
restricted to the UK only. The novelty search was
defined to be a search through the last fifty
years of British patents. This led to patents
being granted in Britain which could not be
granted somewhere else where an invalidating
document existed. It proved increasingly
unsatisfactory for firms actively trading in many
countries around the world to have to deal with
patents valid in one country of importance but not
in others. Thus the concept of absolute novelty
became more attractive and now holds sway in most
of the countries with the most advanced
technology.

However, as a practical matter one cannot switch
from one day to the next from searching fifty
years of UK patents to searching all the world's
literature indefinitely far back. Policy is to
search about sixty years of UK patents, European
and PCT specifications (see 4.1.2 and 5.2) and
also foreign patents from, for example, the USA,
Japan, West Germany or the USSR if the examiner
for that subject knows that in the relevant field
a certain country is a prolific source of patents.
Journal articles, conference reports and other
matter are also collected at the discretion of
each examiner. All material to be searched by an
examiner is classified using the British Patent
Classification and held in one file.

The intention of the examiner is to aim for a
reasonable search, but not to guarantee a
comprehensive one. It is felt that the examiner's
job is to allow the patent if it is not clearly
invalidated by a finding. If industrial rivals
wish to oppose the grant, or later on to challenge
the patent, it is up to them to search more
thoroughly to find additional prior art since they
could be expected to be more familiar with the
sources. This is arguably a dangerous attitude to

take, as it allows a desire to save money to dictate the quality of the search. All searching is a compromise between time and money on one side and completeness on the other. The more comprehensive a file, the longer it takes to search it, including identifying and discarding the false drops, and the more storage space and document handling facilities are required.The US Patent Office is one which carries out very thorough searches. They are developing a paperless, fully electronic documentation system which should ease these problems.

Exemptions from the novelty rules

A point that causes much confusion among amateur inventors and among scientists is their failure to recognise that, ideally, no external communication of an invention should occur before the priority date of the patent. In the US, publication or demonstration at a conference is allowed to take place up to one year before a patent is applied for without invalidating it. In the United Kingdom under the 1949 Act, publication in a learned society's journal was allowed up to six months before the priority date. But under the 1977 Act the only possible exemption is for display at certain approved international exhibitions up to one year before the priority date (13). The list of exhibitions is a very restricted one and a prospective patentee should make very certain, by checking with the relevant section of the Department of Trade and Industry, that an exhibition is covered before making any disclosure. It is safest to assume that nothing is covered and to apply for the patent first.

Inventive Step

This is often called non-obviousness. If an invention is obvious,that means it was a natural thing to try in light of the prior art. In such a case there is no inventive step, no display of true inventiveness, and a patent should not be granted. This is a very subjective criterion but in order to reduce the level of subjectivity it is decreed that an inventive step must be present, but the height of the step, the amount of inventiveness, is not to be ascertained.

As with novelty, the possibility of obviousness is judged against the prior art available before the priority date of the present application, but the prior art is applied with discretion. The examiner is looking for an invention or a line of development either in the same technology or in another field from which analogies can clearly be drawn. The inventor is assumed to be well read in his own and related technical fields. Since only documents an expert in the art could be assumed to have read will be considered, neither unpublished earlier patent applications nor documents of limited availability or in obscure languages are included in the prior art unless there are reasons why the hypothetical skilled craftsman should have considered this particular literature. For instance, when looking for techniques for building structures in frozen ground, one would expect the hypothetical skilled craftsman to find important material in the Russian and Canadian literature. Another way in which an invention could be reconstructed from the prior art is by "mosaicing"; the combination of several documents from different sources which make up components of the invention. This is not permitted unless it would be natural for the skilled man to read such documents together.

It is clear that the element of subjectivity in any judgment as to what constitutes obviousness is very high. Although the examiner is not allowed to use knowledge gained since the priority date with hindsight, it is almost impossible to put oneself back into a position of ignorance once a number of years has passed as may be required in litigation. The criterion of inventive step has manifested itself as a very heavy filter, keeping out all the multitude of small scale advances on which day to day progress depends and which, in practice are not obvious however much they may appear to be in theory. When obviousness was merely implicit in the Statute of Monopolies, the filter was applied less routinely and more workshop level inventions got through.

In English law the question of obviousness is kept as far as possible to the one simple question with "obvious" having the normal meaning of "very plain". In West Germany the practice is to formulate many sub-questions, indicia of obviousness, intended to make the decision more objective. A recent study listed nineteen indicators. Of these the four most useful are whether:

1. the invention overcomes technical difficulties,
2. it satisfies a long felt want,
3. it overcomes technical prejudice, and
4. it embodies an unexpected technical advance.

Questions of obviousness are best explained with reference to examples. English case law is rich in them but they all relate to the Patents Act 1949 and earlier statutes. Although examination for obviousness was only introduced in PA77, the concept has been treated by the courts as being inherent in the phrase "new and useful invention" used in the Statute of Monopolies. Allegations that an invention is obvious are therefore quite common in the law reports.(See 8.3 for an account of sources of legal information). The allegation would be made either at a post-acceptance opposition hearing (see 4.2.1) or after grant in a court case concerning validity of the patent and its possible infringement. PA77 basically codifies the earlier case law, much of which remains valid. However, the possibility of a change of emphasis does have to be borne in mind, in particular since PA77 has to be interpreted in line with the European Patent Convention (see 4.1.2). This Convention was framed in the light of a different legal tradition and will probably lead to some changes as the British system meshes with that of Continental Europe and moves away from the Common law tradition it shared with Commonwealth countries and the USA. Taking this change into account, older cases have become illustrative and need to be reconsidered in the light of changes in the law. The underlying principle is that one is not trying to reward inventive merit but to encourage the dissemination and use of new technologies. Many trivial or non-useful inventions may not be obvious. They are best dealt with by market forces. If a product is not useful it will find no market, if it is useful but trivial then it will have to compete with non patented alternatives.

Inventions which are merely a combination of known objects with no working relationships between the parts could be argued to be novel by virtue of their collocation, but, if each component does only what it is known to do anyway, then the combination would be found to be obvious and thereby unpatentable. For instance, an especially compact fridge, hob and sink unit for a small flat may not have been designed in a particular way before, but could only be patented if a problem had to be overcome. If there were difficulties with the insulation between hob and fridge, this might qualify as a problem, but if the parts all function separately, and no facilitating devices are required, then there is no patentable invention.

Qualifications of the notional skilled person

The person skilled in the art is assumed to possess average technical skills and to know all about a subject but display not even a scintilla of inventiveness. If, in the real world, a number of skills are required to conceive one invention then presumably various experts would work in a team. Outside experts could be called in to solve a particular sub-problem if this required a distinct set of skills. In all these cases the particular expertise required would be assumed to vest either in one person or in the composite expertise of a team. This second assumption would be made only if a subject were too new and complex for one individual to be able to cope with all of it. A case in point concerned the development of colour television where the addressees were regarded as the technicians of the team rather than its leaders whose knowledge was regarded as exceptional (15).

Extent of the prior art

Normally the literature is taken to be that which a diligent searcher would be expected to find. Information published only in a difficult language, Russian say, might be excluded. But if, for instance, the topic were behaviour of building foundations subject to permafrost, on which Russian scientists are known to have done a lot of work, then a search of Russian literature would be expected.

Nature of the problem

To some extent, the answer to the obviousness question is predetermined by the way in which the problem is perceived.

The method used in a number of continental

European countries, in particular West Germany, is to pose a specific question and explore the solution. In Britain a far more empirical approach is used. Many inventions are a "voyage of exploration", the inventor trying to make progress in a specific technology but not necessarily seeking to answer a specific question. Since cases representing both approaches can be found in English case law, both must be presumed to be valid ways of proceeding. It is important, therefore, not to try and force problems into a strait jacket.

An example of a problem and its solution was **Johns Manville's Application** (1967) (16). A filtration process recently invented in the paper industry was applied to produce cement. The problem of filtering the dross out of a cement mixture was well known to skilled craftsmen in that art. There was an article on a new process for doing so in a pulp and paper journal. It was held that a cement technologist thinking about this problem would read this journal and it was then obvious that the process would be worth trying for cement. Therefore the application was refused.

This approach needs to be contrasted with that of the **Amoxycillin** case. Beechams pharmaceutical company was investigating synthetic penicillins (17). They made and patented a whole group of compounds called ampicillins which included amoxycillin, none of which seemed to have any particular advantage.In subsequent testing it was discovered that pure amoxycillin had a particularly high absorbence rate in the stomach. Therefore a separate patent for amoxycillin was applied for. It was held by the Court of Appeal that the invention was only obvious if one were looking for a more absorbable version of ampicillin. However, Beechams were not looking at any one property in particular, they were merely exploring. In this case the invention was held to be non-obvious and a patent was granted.

Selection Patents

The Amoxycillin case just described draws attention to a special category of patents called selection patents. The group of compounds called ampicillins was patented and then the specific compound amoxycillin was also patented. How can one obtain two patents for one compound and why (if at all) is this desirable?

The second patents are called "selection patents", patents issued for a subgroup within a group which is already patented. This subgroup may consist of only one item but will normally be a self-contained group within the larger entity. Selection patents are issued when a subgroup can be clearly distinguished within the larger entity and all members of this subgroup have an unexpected property not found in the members of the rest of the group. In the case of amoxycillin it was one chemical out of a small group. Normally the selection is of a small set of chemicals out of a larger one rather than a single compound.

The practice originated with chemical patents and is largely confined to them. The chemical industry began with substances which reacted with inanimate matter such as dyestuffs. There, if one substance was a good dye then all its analogues, made with other elements from the same columns of the periodic table, would also be good dyes. One or two analogues would be made and then the whole series claimed in a patent. Those made are described as examples and the rest are taken on trust. Chemical formulae written so as to encompass an entire series are usually referred to as "Markush" formulae after the American chemist who first applied for a patent of this form.

Unfortunately, the same system of claiming analogues was taken over and used for pharmaceutical, herbicidal and similar patents. Because their operation depends on interaction with the metabolism of living organisms, the analogues do not behave in a predictable manner and desirable properties cannot be guaranteed. The patentee can still claim an entire series of compounds, but the only ones given secure protection are those which were actually made and cited in examples. This requirement increases the number of examples given but does ensure that the properties of these particular compounds are known and documented. Analogues with the same properties will also be protected. If later on one or a number of the analogues are made and found to have special properties which were not predictable from the knowledge already gained, then the making of these compounds is regarded as a separate invention and a selection patent may be granted. In principle, selection patents could be granted in any field but in practice properties are better understood and more predictable in other subject areas, so that unexpected properties are highly unlikely to be found in a subset of a known group. The attitude of patent examiners tends to be restrictive, they do not wish to inhibit routine extensions of known technology by attaching monopolies to every advance. A commercially valuable discovery is not necessarily an invention.

The attitude of patent examiners to non-chemical discoveries is best illustrated by an example. The patent application of Anglian Water Authorities in 1983 concerned a superstructure to be used under water (15). The original patent said that any extrudable substance would be suitable for making the superstructure. However, when plastic was used it was too light and floated, when steel was used it was heavy enough but sand stuck to it and silted up the passageways. Finally aluminium was found to be suitable just by empirical, trial and error testing, and a selection patent was applied for. All the criteria for a selection patent were there and on purely legal reasoning one should have been granted. But the Patent Office ruled that the list of possible extrudable substances was short and that technical reasoning would indicate that aluminium was a good substance to try. Therefore no patent was granted.

This example illustrates the major disadvantage of patents as a source of technical information. The useful facts are often obscured. The patent is normally applied for as early as possible in the lifetime of an invention and may not be specific enough because necessary work has not been done. In this case "any extrudable substance" was claimed, but the constraints were such that only a few substances would be suitable.

Industrial Applicability

This, the third general criterion of patentability is really the least onerous nowadays. The requirement is that the invention must be capable of industrial production or exploitation which is interpreted broadly as producing a vendible product. This can include a product, a way of

49

making it, a testing method, a way to control manufacture or a way to prevent deterioration. Inventions can be made at any stage of the production process and if they are saleable to those who operate production processes, they are vendible products and are therefore of industrial utility.

At one time agricultural inventions were not regarded as possessing an industrial character and were not patentable under this requirement. However, the attitude nowadays is that anything produced for sale is an industrial product. Where a saleable product is not allowed to be patented, the reasons are usually regarded as being a facet of public policy. This attitude is expressed clearly in **Wellcome Foundation's Application** (1981), a case argued in New Zealand (19). The case concerned a known drug with an unexpected new medical application. The reasons why this should or should not be patentable were set out at great length. There seemed to be no logical reason not to grant a patent. Its ultimate refusal was justified as an expression of public policy.It is always open to Parliament to enact new legislation if policy is to change.This is not a job for the courts.

Non-patentable Subject Matter

Certain matter is specifically excluded from patentability for various reasons under Section 1(2) of PA77. Some material is new but not an invention. Other categories are deemed to be non-patentable whether or not they are inventions.

a)   Not inventions

(i)   A discovery, scientific theory or mathematical method. Theories and methods are ideas, not products. If a discovery results in a product, for instance a new mineral, this is regarded as a product of nature. A patent would only be available if a process had to be applied to produce the product from a substrate so that the final product was not something available in nature.

(ii) Aesthetic creations. These are protected under the laws of copyright and designs registration. As their originality resides in the mode of expression, copyright and designs protection is more appropriate for their needs. This is because it is the depiction of the idea that is being protected rather than its exploitation.

(iii) A set of rules or a method for organising mental activities such as a scheme for doing business or playing a game. These are not products in their own right but ideas for products and therefore not patentable. This category expressly includes computer programs. Only the scheme or program viewed as a set of instructions is non-patentable. If the instructions can be made integral with the mechanical operation of a device, then the entire device can be patented with the program treated as part of the mechanism. In this way, the CAIRS program, a popular in-house information retrieval package, has been patented as an arrangement of electrical circuitry which allows information to be stored in a smaller space, more densely packed than before. A disadvantage of this approach is that the program is protected only in the context of the given application. Copying in another context may not constitute an infringement of the patent.

(iv) The presentation of information. This is not a direct input to an industrial process. Like a set of rules, information is seen as a precursor of a product and is therefore not patentable. An example of an unacceptable proposal is as follows. A conventional magnetic tape cassette had one of its guide poles coloured to facilitate assembly. This was rejected for a patent claim as being a mere presentation of information. Subsequent claims to the method of assembly were then rejected as being obvious.

b) Treatments and diagnoses

As already stated, most barriers to industrial applicability have been removed. However, as a matter of policy this restriction still applies to treatment of the human or animal body by surgery or therapy or diagnoses practised on the body. Substances and apparatus for use in treatment or diagnoses are patentable, it is their application to the processes of medical and veterinary treatments that are not to be monopolised.

The PA49 was in this respect rather informal. Internal treatment of the body was allowed for animals only, but cosmetic and contraceptive procedures were allowed for human beings on the grounds that these were not treatments in the medical sense. A hair strengthening process was regarded as being cosmetic (20) and a regime for taking contraceptive pills was also held not to be a treatment (21) as there was no malfunctioning of the body to be corrected. The boundaries of what was acceptable were left for case law to define. An example of a treatment which was allowed, as it was used on animals only, was Swift's patent which was allowed for the introduction of a meat tenderizer into the bloodstream of farm animals just before slaughter (21). In the PA77, the treatment of both the human and the animal body are explicitly excluded. It is unclear just how much difference this will make. The Swift application would presumably not be allowed but inventions involving cosmetic and other non essential treatments would probably continue to be classified as non medical and be accepted as patentable.

In most common law countries the rule is ad hoc, based on previous case law and general statements about inventions and industrial applicability. The case brought by Wellcome Foundation in New Zealand has been mentioned in previous paragraphs. The conclusive argument in the NZ Court of Appeal was that no explicitly medical treatments have been patented and that such a step should first be sanctioned by the legislature. This so far has been the position on common law countries; that changes should be made by Parliament not the courts. However, the different approach taken to law making in continental Europe is having its effect in the UK. The EPO has allowed a case of second medical treatment by default in that the Convention and its legislative history show no intention not to allow it (22). British law is required to be interpreted as identical to European law as far as possible. This has led to one UK High Court decision in favour of a second medical application even though it was not the way in which the PA77 would normally be interpreted (23). It remains to be seen whether our higher courts will uphold this line of decision in subsequent cases.

c) Anti-social behaviour

A patent will not be granted for an invention which would involve unacceptable behaviour. Behaviour for which the only objection is that it would contravene UK law is disregarded as the patent may be intended to defend exports only. The clause would presumably catch such devices as an improved mechanism for letter bombs.

d) Living organisms

A patent will not be granted for any variety of animal or plant or any essentially biological process for the production of animals or plants. Micro organisms and microbiological processes are not included in the prohibition.

In the USA plants can be patented, and plant patents are numbered in a special series. In Britain and most other countries, including the USA, plant breeders' rights over the seeds or other reproductive parts of new varieties are protected by separate plant varieties legislation. The actual plants are not protected. Animal breeds are not protected anywhere.

This position of not protecting living organisms can be viewed within a logical and consistent framework except where micro organisms are concerned. Natural phenomena of an inanimate kind are not protected and living organisms are products of nature. With micro biology, the problem is one of how to define micro organisms and under what circumstances they are patentable. Micro organisms are approximately defined as being very small independent units visible only under a microscope. Those found naturally are not patentable but, as soon as human intervention has determined their character, protection is allowed.

Products of the techniques of genetic engineering are considered to be man-made on the assumption that they have not developed independently and undetected in the wild. Naturally occurring micro organisms can also be patented if they have been purified into a single-strain breeding culture. It is argued that the pure culture has a different effect from the impure natural one and the intervention of man was required to obtain it.

Genetic engineering patents are becoming very important now. Basic process patents for cutting and splicing genes are held by a number of large American universities either alone or in conjunction with companies which either funded the basic research or were set up specifically to exploit the patents. Licence revenue from the use of these processes will provide a substantial income for the patentees but, the existence of restrictions on such basic tools is likely to inhibit research to some extent and is thus a rather mixed blessing.

Patents for purified versions of naturally occurring organisms have a long history. Louis Pasteur obtained US patent No. 141072 in 1873 for purified brewers yeast when he was advising the French wine making industry. He claimed the yeast as well as the purification method. The equivalent patent was granted also in a number of European countries.

However, there were few such patents until recently. The main consideration given to their patentability has come from America mainly as a result of the Chakrabarty application to patent a bacterium which could degrade oil slicks (23). The bacterium was the result of a great deal of time and money spent on research and development. It being public policy to encourage such work, the investment required is a clear indicator that it is not a simple matter to find and isolate a bacterium. The patent was granted only after the US Supreme Court passed judgment in its favour. The significance of this being that the issue of patents for living organisms was discussed at all levels of the US patent and legal system. A policy was worked out in these hearings which can now be applied to all future applications of this type. Only a statute or another Supreme Court judgment could change this present stance and either would require extensive hearings just as the Chakrabarty case did. The equivalent in the UK would be a case which went to the House of Lords but the amount of discussion generated and the range of issues considered is not so great.

The question still remains, why make a division between micro and macro organisms? There is no logical justification, but techniques of handling and breeding macro organisms are well known and

easily acquired, while those for micro organisms
are difficult to acquire and need expensive
equipment and considerable skill. They are also by
no means self-evident and are still being
developed. There is no legal definition of a
"micro organism". It must be small but need not be
single cell. Probably the need to employ typical
techniques devised for micro organisms will define
the category in practice.

Apart from the normal patenting requirements for
all inventions, those in which a micro organism is
claimed, either as a product or as part of a
process, require in most countries that a sample
of the organism is deposited in a recognised
culture collection. There the cell line will be
maintained and a sample of cells given to any
enquirer as part of the openness of the patent
system. This is necessary because the patent
document which is traditionally intended to
facilitate reproduction of the invention it
describes, cannot provide a description sufficient
to produce an organism. In such cases, a sample
must be given in the interests of full disclosure.
This topic is described further in Section 5,
Chapter 1.

To sum up, any invention is patentable if it
possesses the three qualities of novelty,
inventive step and industrial utility apart from
certain exclusions. These relate to treatments and
diagnoses, anti-social behaviour and living
organisms. PA77 also specifies certain creative
items that are not inventions and therefore also
not patentable. These are discoveries and
theories, aesthetic creations rules or algorithms
and presentation of information.

The Application Procedure

Application

Application for a patent is made on a simple form
which does no more than request that a patent be
granted (24). It must be accompanied by the
specification describing the invention although
the claims may be filed later. The applicant has
to show entitlement to the invention. If he is not
the inventor, he must state his right to the
patent, for instance by being the inventor's

employer. If there is more than one inventor, all are entitled to be listed as inventors and must agree to the application.

The application may be an original British application, or it may be an application within twelve months of the priority date made under the International (Paris) Convention. Original British applications under the PA49 give no priority details. Under the 1977 Act it is made clear that this is the "priority application". "Convention applications" stem from a priority application made within the previous twelve months. This will often be from another country, but it is equally possible to submit a British application claiming priority from an earlier British application. This happens because a patent is normally applied for at the earliest possible moment in the life of an invention, especially when there is a real risk that others are working on the same ideas. Further development work and discussions with users or manufacturers may change the perspective on an invention, which aspect of the invention is producing a change of mind as to the most significant component, or what problem has been solved in the light of the prior art. Such changes may be written into the application only by making a fresh start. However, only those aspects covered in the earlier one will have the earlier priority date and a document may end up with two or more priority dates. Within the twelve month priority period and before requesting further processing, an applicant is free to make any additions he pleases to an application within the normal constraints of novelty and non obviousness. If the specification does not include claims and an abstract when first submitted, these will also have to be submitted within the first twelve months.

The Official Journal: OJ(P)

The Patent Office publishes an Official Journal for its patents section once a week. There is another Official Journal for trade marks. In the OJ(P) new applications are listed. Only brief details are given: name of the applicant, title, application date and number and priority details. There is enough detail to enable a searcher to maintain a general watch for particular subjects or particular applicants and then await further information.

Preliminary Examination and Search

If no further action is taken, the application lapses after twelve months. If the application is to continue, a form requesting search together with a search fee must be submitted.

First a preliminary examination for formalities is made. This ensures that the application contains all essential components; ie an inventor, at least one claim, a description, title, abstract and so on. An approximate assessment of subject matter is made and classification terms assigned. On this basis the application is assigned to an examiner for the search.

A Patent Office examiner holds a science degree and may have joined the service immediately after graduating; he may, however, have some work experience. In the Patent Office examiners specialise in a particular area of technology for a number of years so that they build up a good knowledge of the state of the art. They become highly specialised and do not change their areas of work very often.

When an examiner receives a specification he reads it with sufficient care to understand what is being claimed. He then searches the prior art (as defined earlier) to find documents which might have a bearing on the novelty or obviousness of the claims. The searches are done mainly manually via the British Patent Classification (BPC). Patents of other countries and non-patent documents included in the examiners' files are also classified using the BPC for ease of searching.

Some of the documents selected will contain background information to help the examiners achieve a deeper understanding of an invention. Others will be chosen either because of some similarity to the invention in which case they bear on obviousness, or because they seem to cover the same material as the invention, in which case they could be said to have anticipated it and the invention would not then be novel. At this stage the examiner expresses no opinion about the documents, they could show that the invention is not novel or is obvious, but he has not yet spent time considering whether this first impression is justified. So he writes a letter to the applicant or patent agent listing the documents but not commenting upon them.

Continuations in part and patents of addition

The examiner can comment at this stage on the invention itself in a limited way. If there appears to be more than one invention described, then only the first or the main invention will be searched. He will recommend that subsequent inventions are put into separate patents. These will be fully independent self-sufficient patents but are labelled "continuation in part of number..." to indicate their relationship.

It sometimes happens that later material may be submitted in a patent which cannot stand alone because of the relevance of revelations in an earlier patent. In such a case under PA49 a "patent of addition" could be granted. This patent had only the lifetime of the main earlier patent and if the earlier one lapsed or was revoked, the patent of addition also came to an end. This procedure protected inventive but closely related material developed sometime after an earlier invention. Unfortunately it did not find favour with other European countries when the EPC was drawn up and was dropped in PA77.

Non-Patentable Subject Matter

The examiner can refuse to carry out a search because he feels that the invention is not patentable. This is a matter of interpretation of the specification which could take place at the preliminary examination or more likely at the time of the search. If the interpretation concludes that there is nothing to patent, then no search will be carried out.

Search Report

In the normal course of events the list of documents found in a search will be reported to the applicant and will also be listed in the "documents cited" section on the front page of the specification. Other front page information is added by the examiner in preparation for

The Patent Grant

publication.

Early Publication: The A Specification

Every patent application is published eighteen
months after the priority date or as soon
afterwards as is practicable (25). The text of the
application is published as it was written by the
applicant, but with the addition of front page
information. This publication is irrespective of
the subsequent grant or rejection of the patent.
It is called "early publication" because it takes
place before the substantive examination. If an
applicant decides to withdraw, publication can be
avoided. However, documents enter the queue four
or five weeks before publication and removal
thereafter is not permitted.

The examiners must ensure they have the search
done by the date of publication. When the PA77
publications started, there were long backlogs
built up while PA49 processing was completed.
Therefore most searches were carried out at the
time limit rather than with generous time to
spare. The applicant receives the report and in
many cases publication was automatic because
preparations started soon after the report was
delivered and before the applicant had time to
consider his response. More recently numbers of
applications have fallen and the backlogs have
been mastered so that in 1985 the average time for
the search report to be issued was three months
after the date of filing (25). This great
improvement has taken place in only the last two
to three years. As a consequence, applicants now
do have time to consider their search reports
before early publication. Apart from withdrawal,
the applicant can also amend the description or
the claims in the light of the findings and
amended claims would be published alongside the
original ones.

In practice, nearly all applications are published
in their original form irrespective of their final
destiny.

From the point of view of an information seeker
this is very valuable. It means that descriptions
of the basic ideas of inventions will be
published, whether or not a patent is granted.
Inevitably, there will be a great many

intellectually or commercially worthless ideas published. There will be descriptions of simple ideas that may never be patented because they are (in theory) obvious because they are so very straight- forward. This does not stop them being useful in practice and being not at all obvious to preoccupied and busy technicians. Those ideas which are patented are available first in their unexamined forms. These descriptions might overlap with the prior art and therefore give information which is already in the public domain. In the granted patent much of this will be removed. It is also true that sometimes the examiner will elicit a clearer description than that first provided by the applicant, and then the granted patent will be more informative than the original application.

It is not permissible to add new material to an application when amending it during examination because the limits of what might be protected should be known to all from when the patent is first published. Therefore the information content will not increase and may well decrease after the first publication. For this reason it is usually the application which is the more useful of the two publications for an information seeker.

Documentation

At the date of early publication,apart from the complete specification itself,two items are published: a note in the Official Journal and the front page of the complete specification. In the Official Journal all applications published in a week are listed in numerical and classified order for easy subject scanning.The front page is published as part of the complete specification. It is also published as a separate item because the abstract, drawing and bibliographical information are a useful tool for searching independently of the text of the specification.The front pages are collected in 25 groups of related topics together with name and subject indexes. Each group is defined as a set of adjacent headings of the British patent classification. The sets of headings form approximately self-contained technical fields, and these volumes of front pages and indexes are excellent tools for an initial search (27).

From the date of early publication, the official

file associated with the application is also open to public inspection. This collection, which contains all correspondence, comments and details of any amendments is called the file wrapper.

Substantive examination

The applicant has six months from the date of early publication in which to decide whether to continue with the application. In order to continue, he must submit a form requesting substantive examination and enclose the appropriate fee.

When the examination is to be carried out, the application is referred once more to an examiner on the basis of its classification. Unless the classification is radically changed, the application will go to the same examining unit. It will often be dealt with by the same examiner who carried out the search, but need not be. The examiner will read the specification and compare it with the material cited in the search reports and draw conclusions about lack of novelty or obviousness. He will also consider other aspects of patentability such as whether the invention is intrinsically unpatentable or whether there could be more than one invention included in the patent (unity of invention). All decisions are made focussed specifically on one or more of the claims. The text of the specification is regarded as amplifying and explaining the claims, but the resulting patent will be valid or not judged claim by claim.

The examiner writes to the applicant with his comments and is then prepared to discuss the issues by exchange of letters and telephone conversations or by personal interview with the applicant. As there are no working models involved, a visit is not really necessary and is rare. If a patent agent is employed he will deal with all these arguments on the applicant's behalf.

Apart from his own assessment, the examiner is obliged to consider the representations of third parties. They cannot take part in the examination procedure, but anyone can write to the Patent Office with observations from any time after the application has been published. In this way the examiner learns about more obscure pieces of prior art and also about any demonstrations or public use of the invention before the priority date. Thus the examination consists of a reasoned argument about objections to a patent. If the applicant concedes a point, there might be an amendment to the claims or the body of the specification. This amendment cannot add new matter but it can clarify or restrict the scope of what is already there.

Appeals

If the examiner and applicant cannot agree at any stage of the processing from initial application through the substantive examination, there is an appeals procedure specified in the Act. First there is an internal hearing before an experienced senior examiner. A further appeal may be made to the High Court, Chancery Division, where there are currently two specialist patents judges to hear all intellectual property cases. Their court is called the "patent court". Further appeal to the Court of Appeal is available to any dissatisfied party.This is usually the final stage as an appeal to the House of Lords is only allowed if dispute is over a point of law of general public importance. However, patent litigation tends to be so lengthy and expensive that only really important cases are fought at all so that an application to the House of Lords on a point of patent law has a good chance of being heard. Some patent cases have an extra dimension of EEC interest concerning trade between its member states. The EEC issue is likely to be heard separately from the Patent Act issues through its stages in the various civil courts and may also involve a referral to the European Court of Justice in Luxembourg.

Appeal to any level can result in acceptance or rejection of the application, amendment of the specification or remission to the examiner for further processing.

Second publication and grant

Once the specification is approved, the final document (which defines the content of the granted monopoly) is published simultaneously with the patent grant. The front page information is curtailed, there is no abstract or drawing but the actual specification is complete and in its definitive form. It is called the "B specification" because the "A" following the document number is replaced by "B". The document number remains the same. Second publications are listed in the OJ(P). The entire process should, by law, be completed within four and a half years and the application lapses if not granted by then. In a study of one week of British applications, there were 400 early published specifications. Of these, only 29 did not result in a granted patent and of those granted, 66% of the second publications were substantially identical to the applications (28).

After grant

Once the patent is granted, third parties who were unable to participate in pre-grant procedures can apply to have the grant revoked. They can bring proceedings before the Patent Office or before the High Court. Such proceedings are not normally taken in isolation. If a competitor believes that a patent should not have been granted, he may just ignore it and infringe. It is up to the patentee to prosecute for infringement if he thinks the patent which is presumed valid will stand up to the scrutiny of a court. Then the defendant can introduce a plea for revocation as a counterclaim. Ultimately the patent system works by bluff. Strong patents are respected, maybe after one or two challenges. Weak patents are ignored or, at best, a compromise arrangement is agreed. The cases that are hard-fought in the courts are borderline and there tend to be sound arguments both for and against validity. Infringement is rarely in doubt as patent litigation is too expensive to be undertaken lightly. The system is fair between large companies. Unfortunately, for someone with small means it is very difficult to enforce a patent fully. The owner must either find a backer, bluff convincingly enough to hold-off an opponent or lose and submit to having the idea stolen by a large rival. It is possible to take out insurance for a patent to finance litigation. This is hedged about with protective caveats but is a hopeful development nonetheless.

Renewal fees

The patentee has to pay renewal fees to keep his

patent in force. These are due annually from the fourth year after application or the fifth if the patent has not been granted by the fourth. They rise steeply in value on the principle that only a successful patent should be kept in force for its entire lifetime and if unsucessful should lapse as soon as possible. Also, renewal fees allow the pre-grant fees to be kept lower and thus subsidise the mass of speculative applicants who cannot be sure of the success of their ventures.

Exploitation

The patentee can derive benefit from his patent in a number of ways. He can exploit the invention himself, he can license its use by others, or he can sell it to another individual or an organisation and they will exploit it while the inventor loses all interest once payment has been made. Sometimes patents are obtained to block the progress of rival companies but are not themselves exploited industrially. This situation is not in the public interest and a compulsory licence can be sought for any invention not worked within three years of the patent grant.

In order to encourage liberal distribution of the technologies described in a specification, a patentee has the option of designating his patent as available under a "licence of right". By this, the patentee binds himself to give a licence to anyone who applies for one. Terms need to be agreed between the parties but the patentee allows himself to be bound by terms imposed by the Patent Office if there is any dispute. As a reward for taking up this option, the inventor only has to pay half the renewal fees for that patent.

Information handling aspects

The patent documentation system is self-contained and quite different from the documentation of other forms of technical literature. The deferred examination system has a number of advantages and disadvantages for the information scientist(29).

1) The most obvious characteristic is that two documents, the A and the B specifications, are published for each granted patent. The A specification is likely to contain more information than the B. It is the one used by

searchers because although every grant (B
specification) is associated with an application,
A, not all applications result in a grant. A
proportion of applications are withdrawn or
rejected and there being no granted patent, no B
document will exist. The unexamined documents may
be technically worthless or they may reproduce
material already in the prior art, but often they
will be useful, and may be as stimulating as
granted patents. As previously explained, an idea
may be judged as not novel or obvious, but these
are theoretical and perfectionist concepts, the
description may nevertheless be of value. Under
traditional patent systems no document would have
been published at all and this information would
be lost to the technical general public (30).

2) Since the A specification is normally the more
valuable of the two, it might seem logical for
libraries to keep only patent applications. But,
the B specification also needs to be held in
patent collections so that the extent of legal
protection can be checked by anyone wishing to use
the invention. Therefore patent collections need
to hold two documents where they held only one
before even where the two are substantially
identical. This adds considerably to the storage
problems of patent libraries without much
enrichment of their collections.

3) A problem for inventors is that their secret
is publicised without guarantee of protection.
Once it is realised that no patent will be granted
then there is no protection and yet the idea is
in the public domain. If no application had been
made then the inventor has at least secrecy as a
means of protection. When the Banks Committee in
the 1970s was investigating the previous patent
law, industrialists were asked how they would view
early publication. Their attitude was that access
to the patent applications of their competitors
made revelation of their own worthwhile (31). This
argument is valid for firms with a number of
patents which compete with rival firms. It cannot
apply to small inventors with one-off inventions
who have no compensation for the loss of their
secret if no patent is granted. However, use of
the contents of an A specification is risky
because if a patent is granted, penalties for
misuse will be backdated to the date of early
publication. One should check whether the

application has been withdrawn or refused. There are special provisions for innocent use in the period before early publication (32).

For the information scientist, the lack of protection is irrelevant and the revolutionary aspect is that for every application noted in the official journal, a publication is guaranteed at a definite date. One does not have the uncertainty of the traditional system of not knowing whether or when a specification would be published. For further general considerations of deferred examination, see 4.1.4.

Crown use of patents

Because patents are granted by the Crown, government departments have special rights over UK patents as they act in the name of the Crown. This stems from the time when a patent grant was a privilege from the monarch and therefore the monarch was immune from the restrictions imposed by the patent. Nowadays the degree of immunity of government departments is specified in the Act (33).They are not entirely free of restrictions but have substantial advantages over patent users in general. The PA77 provides that a government department can make use of any patent it pleases provided that the patentee is informed and paid compensation. However, the patentee need not be informed at the time of use. There can be a substantial delay, the moment of revelation and the amount of compensation payable being determined largely by the government. The patentee has only one bargaining counter, that of judicial review. This is a constitutional safeguard by which the reasonableness or otherwise of the actions of any public authority or individual can be scrutinised by the courts. These actions need only to be carried out under powers delegated ultimately by Parliament to come under the umbrella of judicial review.

The exploitation of any patent includes both the making and using of the invention independently or importing it from overseas. The number of patents used in this way is unknown as no records are published but there is a group of civil servants in the Ministry of Defence which reviews all patent applications for usefulness in any branch of government. It is said that quite a number are taken.

PA77 specifically declares the National Health Service to be a Government department for patenting purposes. This is because the only lawsuit reported with regard to the Crown use provisions under the PA49 involved the NHS (34). In 1957 Pfizer held the British patent for a popular antibiotic, tetracyclin. The NHS imported the non-patented generic equivalent from Italy which did not permit any pharmaceutical patents at that time. The import was considerably cheaper and Pfizer sued the NHS which claimed that it was within its rights as a Government department. The case was fought right to the House of Lords which ruled in favour of the NHS. Despite the fact that it won, the NHS did not repeat this exercise elsewhere. The threat of their being able to do so was presumably sufficient to prevent companies overcharging by too provocative a margin.

Patents involving inventions useful to the defence establishment

There is no need for a British resident to apply for a UK patent on his invention. He might wish to apply elsewhere. There are stern warnings on all Patent Office leaflets that for national security reasons, either one must first apply in Britain and wait six weeks before applying elsewhere, or else special permission must be obtained to apply abroad. During the six week interval the Ministry of Defence scrutinises all applications and picks out any it thinks could be useful in the defence industry. They home in on such topics as lasers, high powered computing, cryptography, rocket propulsion and unusual means of transport. Their first selection is very crude, being based on the presence of certain keywords.

The documents are then examined further and many will be released into the system. The few that remain will vanish from sight. A patent may be granted if the invention fulfills all criteria, but it will do its owner no good as it will be secret and only the armed forces could use it. The government will pay compensation under the Crown Use regulations, but this is likely to be substantially less than what would have been earned by civilian and overseas exploitation.If the forces do not use the invention, but use their prerogative merely to block its exploitation, then the owner will derive no benefit whatever.

In general, examples of defence patents cannot be given as they never appear publicly to be identified, but there was recently a case where an applicant "went public" to denounce the injustice he felt had been done to him (35). This concerned an invention in cryptography: the creation of a virtually unbreakable coding system for gaining entry to computer programs and other electronic systems. This would have been very valuable in combating audio, video and computer piracy, and was indeed invented for that purpose. It has now been confiscated by the military and he has no redress.There will be no compensation for loss of earnings.Also there is unlikely to be use as the MOD has its own internal products, so there will be no income at all. It would appear that in certain areas of work it is better to avoid patenting, to proceed to manufacture the product with no protection and to avoid the MOD. In the above case, the man would have made his millions if he had gone ahead without a patent. Unfortunately, it is likely that the firms he was working with would probably have insisted on patent protection for their investments before going ahead with any support even if he had thought of it.

4.1.2   The European patent system

At the same time as the British PA77 came into force, a regional European patent system took effect. PA77 parallels the operation of the bigger scheme. When the new procedure was planned, it was felt that obtaining a patent should be as similar as possible by either route, so as to avoid having two sorts of patent available of different quality. The process of obtaining a patent for the same invention in different countries is repetitious. A search and examination of the worldwide prior art should yield the same results wherever it is carried out and the repetition of this process in many countries is wasteful, both of the applicant's resources and of skilled and highly trained labour. The idea of regional patent systems was borne of the increasing burden of patent work. There are two in Africa (OAPI and ESARIPO, now ARIPO) as well as the European one.

In 1973 the European Patent Convention (EPC) was signed by a large number of West European countries. The Convention was intended to embrace all European countries, not just the EEC. It came into force in June 1978 and has eleven member states. From the EEC there are
  Belgium, France, Italy, Luxembourg, Netherlands, West Germany and the UK.
Other members are: Austria, Sweden, Switzerland and Liechtenstein.

Since Liechtenstein patents can be obtained only in association with Switzerland, there are effectively ten states only. From the EEC, Ireland, Denmark and Greece are missing and look like remaining so for some time to come. Neither Spain nor Portugal are members of the EPC but they have declared their intention of joining as soon as they can.

Application procedure

The EPC required the setting up of a European Patent Office (EPO) which administers the system (36).

The applicant submits his specification either via his national office or directly to the EPO in Munich after defence clearance. The applicant must designate the member states in which he would like his patent to be valid. This can be any number from all of them down to one or two. The number of designated states can be reduced at any time subsequently but it cannot be increased because that would extend protection to a jurisdiction which had thought itself to be free of liability. To limit designations to serious contenders only, there is a designation fee for each country. The fees overall are set to make a European application more economic than separate national applications if the applicant makes three or more designations.

After a preliminary check, the application is sent to the searching branch at the Hague for the prior art search. This part of the EPO originated as the patent collection of the Dutch Patent Office and is still used by them as such. They had a large multi-national collection of patents all classified in one sequence under the Dutch classification. When this became too expensive to

69

maintain in 1947 the Dutch Patent Office organised its transformation into the International Institute for Patents or IIB after the French name. The IIB would maintain the collection and member states would pay a subscription and could either have their official searches done there or could allow nationals to have searches carried out privately. Britain has pursued the second of these options since 1965.

In 1978 the IIB became the searching branch of the EPO. It has to stay in the Hague as this was one of the conditions imposed when the IIB was set up. It still acts as the IIB and carries out searches for non-members of the EPC such as Turkey, Monaco and Morocco.

The prior art search looks for lack of novelty and for obviousness in the same way as the British search, but at the EPO the search is carried out through the patents of a large number of countries and a great deal of non-patent literature, all of which is maintained in comprehensive searching files.Extensive use is made of electronic databases for wide ranging searches.

At eighteen months after the priority date the application is published as it was written. It can be submitted in English German or French, the language of submission being the language in which all subsequent processing takes place. At early publication the claims appear in all three languages.

The search report is put at the back of the specification. It is quite detailed. For every reference cited,the claim to which it is relevant is given and there is a list of codes which indicate highly relevant, partly relevant, or background information.

Examination takes place in Munich to where the file is transferred from the Hague. This means that the examiner will definitely be a different person from the searcher.In fact, to avoid national bias, substantive examination is undertaken by groups of three examiners from different countries. There is one principal examiner who does most of the work, and examination proceeds as in the British Office.

If there are disagreements at any stage, there are no courts to judge the arguments. The national courts of each applicant's home country may have substantial experience in dealing with patents, but no agreement could be reached on the use of these, or on setting up an EPO Court. Accordingly, the entire procedure is kept within the Office. There are boards of appeal of both technical and legal varieties. These are staffed by senior examiners or legal staff, three to each board and from different countries so that the judgments are more likely to follow general trends of European law and interpretation and not be coloured by the national traditions of any single member state. A problem with this is that the boards are all associated with the EPO. There is no neutral third party looking at the technical or legal merits of a case.

Once the application is finally accepted, the patent is granted and published for a second time. The published documents have a number followed by A or B just as the UK specifications do. The designated states are informed that the patent has been granted and they have to accept it as it stands. European patents are not integrated into the sequence of UK patents but retain their own number and sequence and have to be searched separately.None of the member states integrate European patents into their national sequences which would require identification of those which designate that state. For internal use in the British Patent Office, they are given a UK classification and put into the appropriate examiners' files.

All the countries of the EPC except the United Kingdom require that the patent document is translated into their own language before the grant becomes valid in that country. So at the grant stage translations have to be arranged and paid for. This is an advantage for patentees who are less likely to mind paying when the protection is guaranteed rather than at an early stage of application when the result is entirely uncertain as is the case with national applications.

In the UK published European patents appear, like the applications, in any of the three languages with the claims in all three. The only reason the translation provision in the EPC has not been activated is that a few extra staff would need to be employed by the Patent Office to check that translations had been prepared! Groups representing industrial searchers and patent agents have protested at this in light of the usual dearth of language skills in Britain and in the light of the cost to a firm if they do infringe however inadvertently. "Hiving off" the Patent Office may make additional employment easier as the staff will no longer be civil servants. All that would be required is that their costs be covered by fees. However, given an ethos of profit making, it is just as likely that staff costs will be pared down as low as possible.

After grant, the patent is treated as a purely European entity for its first nine months. A third party can bring opposition proceedings against such a patent before the EPO. After nine months the European patent becomes a bundle of national patents. The fees are paid to national offices and rights and duties are all those which attach to national patents (37). Infringement proceedings are always a national matter and do not come before the EPO even during the first nine months.

4.1.3 Variations on the deferred examination system

This is now the most popular patent system. A large number of countries have adopted it. Two variants will be described:

(a) Time scale for processing patent applications

In the Federal Republic of Germany, the Netherlands and the Scandinavian countries the complete process takes much longer. Request for substantive examination can be made up to seven years from the priority date. During this time the application is protected. There may or may not be an official search carried out but the application will be published at the standard eighteen months and from then on the patent office can receive comments on the application. The long gap is likely to eliminate applications which do not result in useful products, and also to allow time for prior art to be unearthed by interested competitors. So the patents granted under this system are likely to protect useful inventions and to be strong patents. The disadvantage is the long time lag which breeds uncertainty as to whether a patent will be granted and allows spurious protection for applications that will not be pursued, or would not be granted.

(b) **Number of publications produced**

The other main variant on deferred examination is the number of publications to be produced.The EPO decided upon two publications: unexamined application and granted patent. The other main model has three publications: unexamined application, examined application and granted patent. There is a formal opposition period between examination and grant where third parties can argue for non-grant of the patent.This system is used by the Scandinavian countries. It was formerly used by the Federal Republic of Germany but the European system has had a standardising effect with member states aligning their national systems to it where this was not too great a change.

4.1.4 Information aspects of the deferred examination system

Advantages

1. The standardised publication of applications at 18 months after the priority date means that all members of a family of applications are published together within a week or two, so a searcher can find details of an invention at a definite early stage. He can also ascertain the extent of the proposed protection as given by family members. An application in the USA (or any other country without early publication) can not be identified until the actual patent is granted.

2. The examiner's search report is usually published which allows an interested reader to study a sample of literature related to an invention. This is not really a feature of the deferred examination system as the USA publishes its search reports, but most countries publish them as part of the deferred examination process so that third parties know what has been found and can confine their comments to additional material. The USA used to be the only country publishing its searches. For countries newly converted to deferred examination, these reports were not

available under their previous systems.

Disadvantages

1. Two or three documents instead of one are published and must therefore be organised and held in libraries.

2. A great many speculative patents are applied for, where the inventions are on paper only and may not work. These often do not reach grant and tend to clog up search files without being of technical value.

4.2   Traditional Patent Systems

The previous main patent system in the world was the traditional one which evolved slowly from when patents were first thought of up to the present day.The first example is the UK 1949 Patents Act, important because patents granted under its provisions are still in force and can remain so until the 1990s. The second example is the US system. The US is the one major patent system which has decided to stay with traditional granting methods. A trial was set up in 1965 carrying out deferred examination on a sample of current applications, but the change-over was not approved and appears not to have been considered again.

The essence of the traditional approach is that, once the application is made, the search and examination are conducted in parallel and no details of the specification are made known until the examiner has accepted the application for grant.

4.2.1   The UK Patents Act 1949

The application was noted in the **Official Journal** when it was submitted. The first submission could be a provisional specification as long as the complete specification was delivered within twelve months.

The examiner would carry out a novelty search which was defined as a search of the previous fifty years of British patents. Obviousness was not an examinable criterion. The substantive examination was conducted in parallel with the

PATENT SPECIFICATION (11) 1302268

DRAWINGS ATTACHED

(21) Application No. 32588/70 (22) Filed 6 July 1970
(44) Complete Specification published 4 Jan. 1973
(51) International Classification G03B 31/04
(52) Index at acceptance
    G5R 11B1A 11B1B 11B1Y 11BY 11Y 13X1 13X3
            13Y 14A1 14AY 14Y 15 16B2 16B3 16BY
            16Y
(72) Inventor JAN CARLSTROM

(54) DEVICE FOR SYNCHRONOUS APPLICATION OF SOUND, EDITING AND PRINTING OF CINE FILM

(71) We, INGENJORSFIRMAN G.A., Sundqvist Aktiebolag a stock company organised under the laws of Sweden, of Djuphamnsvagen 3,871 00 Harnosand, Sweden, do hereby declare the invention, for which we pray that a patent may be granted to us, and the method by which it is to be performed, to be particularly described in and by the following statement:—

This invention relates to a device for synchronous application of sound, editing and printing of cine film.

The operations which can be carried out using a device according to a preferred embodiment of the invention are numerous and, in themselves, known. In order to carry out these operations which will be described below, it is necessary to record during filming a pilot tone signal, in known manner, as follows:—

A pilot tone signal is recorded from the camera simultaneously with the shooting of the film and the sound track recording. The frequency of said pilot tone signal alters in relation to changes of the speed of the camera during the shooting. The pilot tone signal is recorded simultaneously with the sound track on a two channel (auxiliary) tape-recorder.

The operations referred to above are as follows:—

The sound recorded on the two channel tape recorder is transferred to a perforated tape, which can be compared with a film strip having a magnetic surface, similar to a tape-recorder tape. The transfer is carried out on a perforated tape tape-recorder, said tape-recorder speed being controlled by the recorded pilot tone signal *via* a servo control (pilot tone amplifier). Thus, the length and speed of the sound-track recorded on the perforated tape will correspond to the length and speed of the film strip. For the editing, an editing table is required, where the projection of the film and the playback of the perforated tape can be carried out simultaneously and synchronously. When the film and the synchronous perforated tape (the dialogue) are edited, a further perforated tape with music and background effects is recorded. Thereafter the film is run through a special so-called studio projector which is running synchronously with a number of perforated tape tape-recorders, thus mixing the various sound tapes to a final sound tape. From this sound tape and the edited film, a copy with optical or magnetic sound track is now produced. Hitherto, for this purpose further expensive equipment for printing the film and copying the sound and adding a sound track were required.

According to the present invention there is provided a device for the synchronous application of sound to and the editing and printing of a film, comprising, in a single unit, a tape-recorder adapted to be used with a multi-channelled perforated tape tape-recorders, track for the film and having a first drive wheel to feed the perforated tape, a film transporter adapted to be used with the film and having a second drive wheel to feed the film, a projecting unit through which the film passes when the film is passed through the film transporter, a first input coupled to the tape-recorder by means of which a sound track for the film can be recorded on the perforated tape, a motor arranged to drive the first and second drive wheels which are coupled electrically or mechanically in order that the film and perforated tape are advanced synchronously, a second input for receiving a pilot tone signal also recorded at the time of filming coupled to a servo-amplifier which is coupled to the motor to control the motor speed in accordance with the pilot tone signal and which is capable of being disconnected from the motor in order that the motor may be operated independently of the pilot tone signal during editing of the film and perforated tapes and also when it is desired to record additional sound on the perforated tape which has not been recorded during filming.

According to one preferred feature the projection unit is associated with a projection

[Price 25p]

search, the literature once found, being immediately scrutinised. Other points concerned with patentability would also be considered and the examiner would reach a conclusion. If the specification was accepted it would then be published. We see an example of the front page in the accompanying Figure. There is far less detail than on a modern front page.

The accepted specification lay open to public inspection for three months. There was no abstract published with the specification but instead the examiner would write an "abridgment" which was published separately as an alerting and searching service. Also the publication was noted in the **Official Journal**.

During these three months, any member of the public who read the specification could bring opposition proceedings against the grant of the patent: this would be a formal hearing in the Patent Office followed if necessary by appeals. Issues of novelty could be raised, based on material other than the fifty years of British patents already searched. This was also the place to raise a claim of obviousness. Any other relevant issue could be raised but it would receive short shrift if already considered by the examiner. Powerful arguments would be required to open up such a topic as whether the subject of the patent were an invention. When the issue had been decided or at the end of the three months, the patent would be "sealed" and would then be in force for a maximum of sixteen years from the date of application.

This style of procedure generated but one patent specification, plus the abridgment. Such abridgments, written by the examiner, were of a uniform and high standard (38). We see that the full work of examination had to be undertaken in all cases. The main reason for proposing the introduction of deferred examination was to enable applicants to withdraw if they had a hopeless case or where they had found that they would be unlikely to be able to exploit the patent satisfactorily even if it were granted.

4.2.2 The US system

This will be described only briefly. It is a traditional system possessing the following main features : application, combined search and examination, then grant and publication.

At application, no details are made known. There is a US **Official Gazette** for patents but only granted patents are listed in it. The examination is very strict and can take a long time. The applicant is required to submit details of all prior art of which he is aware. These are either mentioned in the patent specification or may be listed on a form to be kept on file. Once the examination is completed the patent is published and granted. The patent specification has an abstract at the front but this is not republished in the Gazette. The main claim is given in the Gazette along with bibliographic and priority details. Lifetime is seventeen years from the date of publication. Until recently there were no renewal fees but an amendment brought in in 1981 introduced fees as from 1986. They are set to recover 25% costs and can go up every 3 years. They are due at 3.5, 7.5 and 11.5 years after publication.

At the same time a procedure was introduced for re-examination of patents in force by the Patent Office. This can be requested by the patentee who must give a reason for his request, or by a third party who would take no further part in the proceedings.This route provides a chance to go through complex issues without going to court.

One peculiarity of the US system is that it is the first inventor who is entitled to the patent, rather than he who first reaches the Patent Office. To decide on the inventor requires some careful record keeping. One qualifies to be the first inventor by having had the basic idea and then by having been diligent in reducing this to practice.To have had the idea but then shelved it for some time reduces the protection, since a rival who started later but worked continuously may be said to have done more real inventing. For this reason US companies often keep detailed laboratory notebooks. Each page is numbered and signed and the whole book kept locked in a safe as a daily record of ideas and experiments. Legal proceeding to establish the first inventor are called "interference" proceedings.

In Britain and other countries, the first arrival at the Patent Office, as given by the official date and time stamp gets the priority and the patent.

The US was the first country to publish its search report: just a plain list of patents and other literature cited by the examiners on the front page of the patents.

The US Office maintains its own patent classification. This is placed on the front page and will be dealt with separately in 7.3.

Types of patent

The US sequence of ordinary patents covers inventions in technology whether chemical, electrical or mechanical. There is a separate series of **reissue** patents where the contents remains essentially the same but an error is discovered of sufficient substance that it requires a special examination and reissue of the specification.

Another numerical series consists of **defensive publications.** These are a summary of an invention published to act as prior art and therefore prevent anyone else from utilising it. No positive protection results, only the negative one of refuge from another's inventiveness. An inventor might publish defensively if he felt that the invention was too small or too similar to another or he did not wish to develop it further.

A third series comprises **plant patents.** These protect true-breeding varieties of flowering plants or crop plants.

Designs in the US system are regarded as being closely related to patents. They are published in the **Official Gazette of Patents,** and their classification is integrated with the patent classification having merely an extra "D" for design appended

4.3   The Comecon Patent System

The Comecon countries all have similar systems based on that devised by the Soviet Union after the Revolution. It is a dual system of patents and inventors' certificates which works as follows.

External applicants can apply for standard patents using a system of combined search and examination. The Comecon countries are all members of the Paris Convention which ensures equal treatment for all members. The problem in a centrally planned economy lies in putting the invention into practice. As the state controls all industry, it requires the sanction of the state to incorporate an invention into the production cycle. Because of this, although internal applicants can also apply for patents, very few do. An internal inventor normally applies for an inventor's certificate. This confers recognition of inventorship and usually a small sum of money or some other form of payment based on the social utility of the invention. The rights and duties of exploitation of the invention fall to the state which makes an objective measure of commercial exploitability impossible. External applicants do not apply for inventors' certificates, for them the rewards would not be sufficient incentive. They would presumably have contacts with the state industries to ensure some chance of exploitation. Some of the Comecon countries do allow a certain amount of private enterprise as well.

There is a move to get inventors' certificates included in the Paris Convention so that they confer priority status for patent or certificate applications elsewhere and for outsiders to be able to apply for internal certificates.

4.4   Registration Systems

These are the simplest of all systems. They are used in Belgium, Spain and in numerous small territories which were or are British Colonies or other dependencies such as Malta, the Falkland Islands and the Channel Islands. It was the system used in France up to 1968.

Under a typical registration system, a patent specification is presented to the Patent Office. It is given a formalities check to ensure that all legal requirements are fulfilled. Then the patent is granted automatically. This means that the position of patent examiner does not exist. Requirements as to novelty and inventiveness still apply but the only examination is that carried out by the courts when a patent is challenged and defended. As this only occurs with commercially valuable patents, the effort is focused just where it is required and this is the rationale of the system.

Such systems exist in rather few countries, as courts would be overloaded in those patenting countries which are both industrially innovative and litigious in temperament.

Details of the patent system in any particular country are best obtained from a loose leaf compilation (39). There also exist directories of the official documentation of various patent offices (40).

Chapter 5   International Protection

With the pattern of trading in industrialised countries being predominently trans-national rather than remaining within national boundaries, patents need to be useful in many countries, not just one. Because of this strong common interest throughout the industrialised world, there is efficient international administration of patents and of other forms of intellectual property.

5.1 The Paris Convention of 1883

This Convention was the first in the intellectual property field, its design has been used for many later conventions. Its cornerstone is the principle of **national treatment**: each country will give the same rights and obligations to citizens of other member states as it gives to its own nationals. National sovereignty is not diminished in that each country can choose its own laws, but there must be no discrimination in their application. In this way it was made as easy as possible for countries to join the Union (this being the collective noun for all the states which adhere to that convention).

The second major provision of the Convention was to establish a grace period for applications. If national patent laws all said that an invention must be novel on the date of application, then one would have to apply to all countries of possible interest simultaneously. To get over this and allow time for consideration, many states concluded bilateral agreements; these were unwieldy and repetitive but not identical. To cure this inconvenience, the Paris Convention established a uniform grace period of one year.

The date on which the first application is made is called the **priority date** and other applications made within twelve months will be accorded the same priority date. The first patent document to be published is called the **basic patent,** all the rest are called **equivalents** and the group as a whole is called a **family.** Note that despite being part of a family, each patent is to be considered independently in its own country. Invalidity in one member state does not affect its status elsewhere.

This system of national treatment and recognised priority puts order into the international system, provided that most countries are members. This is approximately the case: about 2/3 of the countries of the world are members and since China joined in December 1984 all important technologically active states are members. The total as of January 1986 is 97 states (41).

In the 1880s there was a general attempt to regulate the exploitation of intellectual property between countries. Following the Paris Convention of 1883 which covered all industrial property, in 1886 in Berne an international Convention was signed concerning copyright. After a few years of independent existence, the administrations of the two Unions were merged into one organisation which nowadays administers these and most other agreements concerning intellectual property. It is a United Nations Organisation situated in Geneva and called WIPO, the World Intellectual Property Organisation.

The Paris Convention has been revised on a number of occasions, never to any great extent. At present with its membership swollen by developing countries which feel exploited (42), there is an attempt to obtain especially favourable conditions for these countries and to curtail the rights of patentees from developed countries when holding patents in less developed countries. This breaks the national treatment ethic and has been opposed by the rich Western nations, in particular the USA. A majority could force these views through but this could well lead to break up of the Union. No action at all might also lead to a break up so there is deadlock at present (43). This trend parallels the setting up of the Universal Copyright Convention by Unesco in 1952. The countries involved did not want to join the Berne Convention as its requirements were too heavily weighted to authors against readers.

5.2   The Patent Co-Operation Treaty   (PCT)

Despite the Paris Convention, there is still a great overlap in the workings of national patent systems. Each country or region has to carry out searches and examinations and administer granted patents. The contents of laws and the decision whether or not to grant a patent remain jealously guarded national prerogatives. One or two supra-national regional systems have been set up but requirements are too diverse for one system to suit the entire world.

The PCT is a procedural Treaty concerned mainly with the literature search. In summary, it provides that a centralised literature search is carried out. This forms the basis upon which each national patent office carries out its own examination. Countries can opt for a centralised examination, but the final decision as to grant always remains in their hands (44). As of January 1986, 39 countries from all six continents were members.

A patent specification is submitted in duplicate to WIPO with a list of designated states. One specification remains at WIPO for publication, while the other is sent to one of a number of national patent offices which have agreed to act as International Searching Authorities. A characteristic of the PCT is that, although it specifies a minimum level of search, only a few patent offices have large enough libraries to achieve this level and they are the ones which carry out the international searches. They were also chosen to reflect a balance of regions and systems. The offices are those of the USA, USSR, Japan, Sweden, European Patent Office, Austria and Australia.

The minimum search is that through the **PCT Minimum Documentation** which consists of all patents published since 1920 in important countries and a selection of key journals which publish material useful for inventors.

The ten patent offices whose patents are included

are those of the USA, USSR, the German Empire up to 1945 and then the German Federal Republic, France, the United Kingdom, Japan, Switzerland, OAPI, EPO and PCT. These being the most prolific countries or regions, it is highly likely that an existing patent of any importance in any other country would have an equivalent published in one of them.

The list of some 160 journals is held at WIPO. These journals are drawn from all over the world; additions or deletions are made at the suggestion of national patent offices. They contain articles on new equipment and techniques and theories which can be added to examiners' files as prior art.

Apart from this substantial minimum documentation, each office is supposed to search any other source which appears of value to it. Thus Japanese, Russian, Swedish and other materials are searched only by the appropriate offices, which introduces a certain non-uniformity into the procedure. This is probably unavoidable.

The literature search which is concerned with both novelty and obviousness results in an international search report which is sent to the applicant. At eighteen months from the priority date, WIPO publishes the application and the search report in a continuous PCT series.

The applicant then has two months after publication to decide whether to continue the processing in all or any of his designated states. To proceed, WIPO sends a copy of the application to the patent office of each state listed. The application then enters each national system for examination and possible grant.

As a variant: if a country is one which has agreed to international examination, the specification will be sent to a patent office acting as an International Examining Authority. A full examination is carried out, based on the relevant national law. A recommendation as to grant will be transmitted to the country or countries concerned. The examining offices need not be the same as the searching offices. The main requirement is for experienced examiners and therefore Britain among others has volunteered. As use and membership of the PCT grows this could become quite a sizeable job, examining for small countries which do not wish to employ their own staff. Such work could be a lifeline for patent offices of only marginal viability such as those in various European countries whose workload and consequent fee income has been depleted by the advent of the European Patent Office.

Apart from the UK, which examines but does not search, examining offices are also searching offices.The choice of examining office is regionally based.It may be the same one that carried out the search or one in the same regional group.

The final decision on acceptance of a specification still lies with each country separately. Any compulsion to accept the patentability of an invention examined in a foreign patent office would strain the principle of national sovereignty, and might deter many countries from joining the PCT.

In many respects the PCT should be treated as an extension of regional patent systems. But it does not grant any patents; it merely unifies some of the steps towards national grant. It is also an extension of the Paris Convention in that, after the eighteen months to publication, there are a further two months before the decision on designated states needs to be finalised. This increases the effective grace period from the twelve months of the Paris Convention to twenty months. It also allows the full time to be used. Under the Convention one has twelve months but the decisions have to be made at about eight in order for an application to be submitted in time. The four months are required to translate the application which includes some rewriting to conform with local requirements.

A further advantage of using the PCT is that of language. The searching authorities will deal with a specification in any language they can cope with. When the application is published, English, French, German, Russian and Japanese are accepted. The abstract and international search report are additionally published in English for non-English specifications. For any other language of application, the specification is published only in an English translation.

Each country will require a translation into its own language for the national phase but, before it does so the one document in its original language with possibly an English translation is all that is necessary. Prior to the PCT, a translation had to be lodged at once with each application.

Thus the twenty month gap allows an applicant more time to consider which countries he wants to proceed in and also allows a deferment of fees. All of this saves time and money (45).

In conjunction with the PCT, WIPO has organised the compilation of a journal of lists of articles appearing in Minimum Documentation journals. These are articles suitable to put into an examiner's search file and are classified by the International Patent Classification. The journal has been published since 1980 on an experimental basis only and distributed free of charge to patent offices world-wide. No final decision on its future has been taken. The journal, called JOPAL - Journal of Patent Associated Literature - is destined to be published and sold on subscription to anyone who wants to buy it as well as being distributed to patent offices.

5.3 Regional Patent Systems

The PCT is a compromise. While it encourages as many contries as possible to join by not interfering with national patent laws, it brings all the different systems into fairly close co-existence.

The next stage, logically, would be to merge laws. Examination procedure depends on the law under which it is carried out. A merger, therefore, of examinations would require countries to operate under identical or at least closely similar laws.

The merger approach is best attempted regionally at least to begin with.

The European Patent Convention, EPC, co-exists with national laws but has had a strong unifying effect as it is awkward for a country to operate its patent system under two similar but not identical laws. In the UK, the new national Act was aligned with the EPC, so there was no problem.

In West Germany, their three-fold publication system was converted to a two-fold one although a time-span of seven years between search and examination is still allowed. The EPC allows only six months between early publication and examination. Thus alignment is partial at best. Belgium runs a registration system nationally but, as this is completely different from the EPC, there is no scope for confusion.

It is not intended to dispense with national patent systems at all as there will always be small enterprises which only want and can only afford very limited protection. But within the EPC it was intended to have a CPC or **Community Patent Convention** in which the EEC is treated as one country within the EPC. This CPC requires not only a common procedure to grant, that of the EPC, but also a common substantive law. For the entire lifetime of the patent, it would be valid in the whole of the EEC with a common law for defining validity and dealing with infringements, and common courts for settling disputes. The Convention has been drawn up but still requires ratification by all members of the EEC (46). To begin with, some EEC members are not members of the EPC and membership is a pre-requisite for joining the CPC. Two are Denmark and the Irish Republic and their reasons for not joining are concerned with wider political considerations: mainly public distrust of "European" organisations irrespective of their merits. The EEC continues to grow; Spain and Portugal and Greece, the most recent members are not members of the EPC either, they are likely to join when their internal patent arrangements are sufficiently well organised. Also, plans for a "mini CPC" for EEC and EPC members have reached an advanced stage (47).

One can see the complexity involved in merging the laws of one region. Whether the CPC will ever come into effect is an open question. Therefore ideas of a "world patent" with one law for all, which is even more remote, are best forgotten.

Chapter 6   Patent Searching

There are four types of searches one can undertake with patents.

6.1 Legal Status

If one wishes to use the invention described in a patent in any way, it is important to know if it is in force within a certain territory and, if so, whether only the proprietor or any licensee is using it. Such information is normally available only at the national patent office of the country concerned.

In Britain the Patent Office maintains an Official Register with the name and address of each patentee, the number and title of each patent and its date of lapse or expiry. A patent lapses if renewal fees are not paid when required (including grace periods for late payment). Expiry occurs when a patent has run for its full term, currently twenty years. In the Register there is also a space for comments. If legal action is taken, this is noted as is any resulting decision which affects the patent such as an order for its amendment or revocation. In the comments section, licences are listed. Notification of licence agreements is compulsory, but often ignored as the penalty is only a small fine. Notification is only essential if the licence needs to be recognised in legal proceedings. Even when notified, only the existence of a licence but not its terms is recorded. Therefore this part of the Register is incomplete. In all respects the Register constitutes the official record and reliance upon it confers immunity from charges arising from incorrect information.

The Register can be consulted at the Patent Office in London in the public search room. A fee is payable for each patent referred to, currently £2 (1986) and the Register is held in a succession of large bound volumes in numerical order. The same fee also entitles a searcher to examine the "file wrapper". This is the file opened when the application is made. It contains successive versions of the specifications, letters between the applicant and the examiner, third party comments and internal Patent Office memos, in short, all documentation relating to a patent application. The file wrapper becomes open to public inspection (OPI) on the same day as the application is published. It can be consulted only on the premises, although documents can be copied.

There are two exceptions to the rule that official records are available only at the national patent office. The Register of the European Patent Office is available online on the EPO's computer and can be received on any terminal capable of communicating via the public telephone lines or IPPS network. The files will be sent by post to the patent offices of member states and enquirers can consult them there. The contents consists of photocopied documents so that the originals always remain in Munich.

The second exception is that INPADOC (see Chapter 8) carries legal status information for eight authorities: Britain, Austria, France, West Germany, Switzerland, Netherlands, EPO and PCT. This is available with quarterly updates on microfiche and available online from the computer in Vienna only. The information is provided and vouched for by the patent offices concerned and is a valuable service.

6.2 Name Searching

This is relatively straightforward. Patents can be searched for by name of patentee or applicant and often by name of inventor. There are two problems.

(a) Alphabetisation

The entries are held in alphabetical order. The rules for alphabetisation are complex and vary from country to country. Standardisation seems to be impossible to agree upon. This means that a company name like "du Pont de Nemours" can occur in different places in different files. The same problem arises with respect to policy for prefixes "Mc" and "Mac", the German "von", the Dutch "van" etc. Unfortunately there is no cross-referencing.

The UK name indexes prior to 1979 are published in volumes of 25000 specifications each covering the published accepted specifications. Since then they cover the published applications of which there are far more and are published annually. Because of the vast increase in output these indexes were converted to computer production and during a period of initial problems they became very unreliable, for instance company names filed under "The" is a major problem. The faults have been corrected but the backlog has not been put right. Because this is a complex task, it is rather uncertain when or whether it is likely to be undertaken.

(b) Patentee/applicant names

The name has to be known precisely before searching. Some organisations have rather strange and unexpected names. For instance the "Food Manufacturers Research Association" at Leatherhead, often called the "Leatherhead Food RA" could be expected under either F for Food or L for Leatherhead. In reality its correct name is "British Food Manufacturing Industry RA" and is under B for British.

Some organisations set up a special subsidiary company to hold their patents. This makes them almost inaccessible to a casual searcher which may be one reason for doing it. For instance the National Coal Board, now British Coal, patents under "Coal Industries".

As a general rule when name searching, if no patents are found when patents are known or expected to exist, one must use ingenuity to search in different places in the name index. It may often be necessary first to search a company directory to ensure that the company name is correct or to distinguish one company from others with similar names.

The normal practice is to search under the name of

the patentee/applicant but where this is a prolific firm, it is useful to be able to search by inventor, and vice versa.

6.3 Family Searching

It is often necessary to trace other members of a patent family starting with one member. This may be either the basic patent (first to be published) or one of the equivalents.

The family relationship is defined by the priority. If a patent carries the same patentee and inventor names and has the same priority country and date, it is the equivalent patent.

At its simplest, family searching is a version of name searching. Starting with the priority year so as to be sure of missing nothing one searches forward. An equivalent should appear in anything between two and five years later, but if none does a searcher can never be sure that it will not turn up much later. Unless there are strong reasons for continuing, ten years is probably a safe upper limit.

Since the early 1970s the need for individual name searches has greatly declined with the compilation of equivalents indexes by various services. These enable one to find the entire family in one list. Such services will be described further in Chapter 8.

Equivalents searches usually fulfil two objectives:

(a) to find the extent of protection of one invention. Widespread protection would indicate strong likelihood of commercial success or at least that the owner is taking exploitation seriously.

(b) to find a version of the specification in a language the requester can read. Equivalents are not precisely identical, but most of the information is there, any differences being not so much of content but of emphasis. The claims are the parts most likely to be altered leaving the main text the same. Therefore unless a specification is to be used for legal purposes, a translation is usually unnecessary if an equivalent can be found.

6.4 Subject-matter Searching

The main characteristic upon which a patent search can be based is its subject matter. Patent offices have always dealt with this by assigning classification codes to classify and index the contents of a specification. Searching takes place through indexes based on these classifications. Patents being a very well defined and separate form of literature, searchers other than patent examiners have tended to use the classifications assigned by the patent offices for their searches and have kept patents as separate collections. Recently with the growth in use of online searching, infrequent users of patents have become able freely to search patent literature using keywords. Patent specialists are also considering this method of searching but in parallel continue to develop and apply their classifications.

The structure of patent classifications and the problems of subject matter searching are dealt with in the next chapter.

Chapter 7   Patent Classifications

These are the key to most present day patent subject searching. Various countries have their own national classifications. There is also an international classification which is used as the sole classification by a number of countries. In others it is printed on specifications so that it can be used but the national office uses its own classification.

The classifications differ in their notation and also in the principle of organisation which must reflect national patent law. They operate a general pattern and follow broadly similar principles just as national patent laws are broadly similar. Therefore the principles can be discussed apart from the peculiarities of each system.

General Principles

Classifications divide up the universe of knowledge in a logical fashion, using principles of division which depend on the use to which the material classified is to be put (48).

For patents the universe is that of all patentable subject matter. The classification divisions are very fine, far more than with conventional library classifications. These are used to list the subject of an entire book or a technical paper. The invention in a patent often relates to changes in a small part of a well known system, and this subtle change is what has to be recorded. Many inventions may be made relating to the one large system and they need to be distinguishable. It is only when an entire new technology is opened up that a new broad term might be introduced,for instance "hovercraft" as a new form of flying machine. Because of this vast detail, all the problems of classification which are known but bearable in libraries are perceived as far greater with patents, the alternatives far more starkly defined than for other types of classification. Thus patent classifications provide a fertile ground for classification research.

The classifications grow entirely empirically. When a term becomes overloaded and much inventive activity is detected in an area, then one or more new terms are created at whatever level of the classification is required.

There are no cataloguing rules for patent literature because classifications are for information retrieval purposes only. On the shelves they are usually in numerical order. When an order is required, the order given in the schedules always seems to be sufficient.

What Is To Be Classified?

The main part of the patent, so far as the Patent Office is concerned, is the actual invention. But this may be in a technology different from the technology of the device in which the invention is incorporated. For instance, extrusion methods for metal-working techniques will be adapted for specific purposes. Or again, a tempered metal for positioning in a blast furnace could be regarded as a metal-working technique or as a component to improve the operation of a blast furnace.

This same problem arises when a component of a device is improved upon, such as the crystal at the centre of a laser. The light is provided by a large crystal of one of several materials and the greater the purity and regularity of the crystal lattice, the more narrowly defined is the beam frequency. A patent concerned with an improved growing method for laser crystals could be represented as an invention in the field of crystallography or in the field of laser technology.

This is a question of how to define what is the invention. It is related to but not identical to a second question.

What is the Principle of Division?

If someone invents a valve, it may be for the control of sewage, beer, water or any other fluid. Its operation will be recognisably that of a valve in all cases. A spool may wind film in a camera or large heavy ropes for securing ships. The spool operation will not differ although the scale and details of its construction will.

Out of this dichotomy, two principles of division have arisen. **Product oriented** classificaton classifies by the industry in which the invention would be used: brewing and sewage equipment and cameras, would all be in different places.**Function oriented** classification classifies by the role the invention plays: all valves are valves, all spools operate using the same mechanism too. Therefore all valves and all spools are classified together irrespective of use. The two methods of classification are not mutually exclusive in that one can have parts of a classification using the functions and parts using the products and cross references between them. The same material can also be both function and product oriented at different depths of the classification. The two types merely represent the extremes.

Many patent laws now require consideration of non-obviousness of an invention. This encourages function oriented classification. A designer of a valve would be expected to look at other types of valve to see if his problem had been solved. Thus all valves should be together to facilitate a search across technologies.

On the other hand, the interest of searchers from industry is to find improvements in the technology of their products. Many different functions can potentially be modified as an improvement but the searcher wants only those relating to his industry. Patents are there to be used by the industrial public as stimulation for further R&D. Firms must also avoid infringing a patent when bringing out a new product: an expensive mistake if they do. Therefore industrial searchers need a means reliably to identify all the patents related to their work. The amount of material produced in related field which could perhaps be useful is so large that R&D staff cannot in practice read it and do not do so unless they have already recognised the topic as a useful one. Thus there is an inbuilt conflict of interests between examiners and R&D staff involved in the construction of patent classifications.

One further general consideration before plunging into the details of individual systems:

Classifications and Indexes

Some "classifications" are pure classification schemes. Others involve indexing as well. The distinctions are occasionally clearly marked out but are usually quite indistinct. Yet there is a clear difference in the type of term and the purpose it serves.

In a **classifying** approach, a large subject is broken down into smaller portions following the logic of a principle of division. A large subject is systematically narrowed down into lots of interrelated components. For instance one might divide as follows:

```
Clocks
   Electrically driven
                  Analog
                  Digital

   Mechanically driven
                  Pendulum power
                  Water power
                  Clockwork
```

The degree of indentation gives the level of division of which there are three in this example. Each split creates a finer subdivision of the subject.

An **indexing** approach would merely note features of interest with no concern for the structure of the subject. Therefore in the example above we could have

liquid crystal display
hands and numbers coated with luminescent material
cylindrical pendulum
hexagonal pendulum

Many classification schemes are mixed, with the

classifying part giving structure in rather abstract form and the indexing part filling in concrete details. It is possible to have a purely classifying or purely indexing scheme. However the different terms have often not been distinguished in the supporting literature of the schemes and their hybrid or pure natures have not been clear to users. It is only in the last few years, with the increasing cost of running these classifications, that a more detailed analysis of the role of different components has been undertaken. This structure will be illustrated in the context of the classifications to be described.

7.1 The UK Classification

In its outermost layers, the UK system is a purely classifying scheme. Once the layers are in place, indexing terms are used at the working level (49).

The universe of patentable ideas is basically the whole of technical subject matter, taking technical in its very broadest sense. This is first divided into eight **Sections** A to H.

    A = Human necessities
    B = Performing operations
    C = Chemistry and metallurgy
    D = Textiles and paper
    E = Civil engineering and building accessories
    F = Mechanics, heating and lighting
    G = Instrumentation
    H = Electricity

Each one of these sections is then divided into **Divisions** which range in number from 2 to 8 for each section. These range from A1 - agriculture and animal husbandry, to H5 - miscellaneous electric techniques. Finally each division is divided into a number of **Headings.** There are about four hundred ranging from A1A - fishing, to H5R - radiology, radiography and irradiation. For each division, the maximum number possible would be 26. They range from 2 to 24 in practice and it is fairly rare for an entirely new heading representing new subject matter to be added. As an example of the degree of novelty required for a new heading, hovercraft were given one as being too distinct from other flying machines to share their heading. However, the letters are spaced in such a way that a new one could be slotted in at many points throughout the schedules. Thus division A6, entertainment, splits into

       A6D outdoor sports
       A6H indoor games
       A6M amusement and exercising apparatus
and   A6S toys

There are wide gaps in notation between headings so that additional entries may be made. The entries could be new ones or be existing headings transferred from elsewhere as part of a revision. If a classification had no built-in flexibility like this it would soon become muddled. There are two reasons for creating new headings. One is that a new area of technology has come into being, such as the hovercraft. The other is that relationships between areas of technology change, and these changes must be reflected in the relationships between the headings.

The headings are the working level of the classification. The Patent Office has available approximately one examiner per heading; they assign classifications within the heading and carry out most official searches using it. Because of their experience with their headings, the relevant examiners are fully consulted when the classification comes up for revision in a particular area and are often instrumental in determining the details of the revised version.

Further sub-divisions below the heading level have no structure and are merely called **Terms**. There are as many as are required at each level and have developed by accretion in a totally pragmatic manner in that when a term becomes overused it is split into two or more finer sub-divisions. No theory of knowledge guides the splitting at this stage, it is merely the rate of inventive activity. These accretions are in turn synthesised through consolidations and occasional re - organisations from the Classification Section. It is at the term level that the scheme splits into classifying terms and indexing terms.

The present scheme for the UK classification dates from 1963. Prior to that the scheme was quite different. Between 1963 and 1978 the classification had no distinct classifying and indexing terms. The classifiers used a broadly indexing approach in that they tried to note features of interest whether these formed a part of the invention or not. In practice, once the examiner had defined the invention he would select an appropriate heading and index items of interest within it. A second heading could represent a different aspect of the invention, but going beyond a heading only to correlate with non-inventive features or with applications was discouraged. To this extent the classification was restricted to one viewpoint but, as applications and characteristic features were catered for under each heading, entailing considerable redundancy, this was not a serious restriction. During this period the UK classification gained a good reputation as a precise and accurate searching tool for industrial searchers.

However, the detailed classifications were time-consuming to assign and created much material to search through. An examiner would conduct a search on terms within a heading and then flip through the specifications he found checking for relevance. They were finding too great a proportion of non-relevant items.

Therefore since 1979 the classification has been streamlined. The terms are grouped as either classifying terms or indexing terms. The classifying terms are used to denote the technology of the invention. These are function oriented whenever possible so that related inventions in different technical fields will be found together. The indexing terms enumerate other items of interest, either not directly concerned with the invention or concerned with the technology of the application. A majority of these changes were introduced with the 1979 "Edition A" of the classification. Others have been brought in gradually since then and a few were introduced beforehand.

The main impetus for this change was the introduction for all patents of the search related to obviousness of an invention. For a novelty search, the target is the same invention and, the more detail in which it can be described, the better. The search for obviousness requires finding advances in parallel technologies. Therefore the classification has to be arranged differently in order to be sure of finding these technologies.

The arrangement and contents of the terms is best illustrated by examples as follows.

Examples

Consider the heading A4K = Brushes etc.
Brushes are defined as "devices having a plurality of bristles or like flamentary elements which, by a form of a scraping action introduce material to or remove material from a surface, or arrange hair or the like into desired formations".

The classifying schedule is arranged hierarchically, each level of the hierarchy being indicated by dots for the level of indentation. The terms are given by letters only.

A4K Brushes etc

    associations of brush parts for unit functions

KDA . for relative rotation of bristles

    . association of bristles with other parts or functions

KDB . . mounting or fixing bristles

Note that the terms are written out as "A4K DA" and "A4K DB".The "K" is not repeated except as a reminder on the pages of the schedules. The dots give the position in the hierarchy. "Associations of brush parts for unit functions" is the highest level, but is not a term assignable to documents as there is no notation. **KDA** and **"association of bristles"** are at the same level and **KDB** is one step further down subsumed in **"association of bristles"**.

Next to each term, a term frequency number is given, showing how often any one term has been assigned. In the introduction to each heading, the operative date for term frequencies is given. Many go back only to Edition A in 1979 while others extend much further. This depends on how far back the examiners' files have been reclassified. The term frequencies show how often

a term has been assigned and therefore how useful
it is to search it. A term assigned too often
might produce a broad field of documents which
have to be cut down by use of other terms. A very
rarely assigned term may be unduly restrictive but
in some circumstances may be just what is
required. Term frequencies are of limited use only
and it requires skilled judgement to apply them
properly. Within these limits they are very
valuable.

Indexing schedules are associated with specific
classifying terms. They consist of numbers only.

Indexing terms associated with A4K DB are

    K201 by adhesive, soldering, brazing, melting
    K201 by twisted wire
         by clamping or crimping-
    K203 . bristles held in U shape with free ends
    K204 . bristles held at one end only
    K205 . other aspects of clamping or crimping
    K206 by other means

This is the entire indexing schedule associated
with KDB. Inventive activity in this area is not
very great so there is no need to make additional
subdivisions.

Applications: The Universal Indexing Schedule U1S

The classifying terms are abstract and function
oriented where possible. Often the applications
of an invention are not obvious from the assigned
classifying terms. One of the worst offenders here
is "coated products". An example of this is a
carbon coating invented to coat an artificial
heart valve and make it more acceptable to the
body. This was classified only under "coated
products" and became lost to any searcher looking
for advances in artificial organs (50).

This is a serious problem and the community of
industrial patent searchers put much pressure upon
the Patent Office. They have responded with a new
approach to the problem. A new heading was
created: U1S, the Universal Indexing Schedule, in
which applications and properties are listed in a
general way to be applied to all inventions,
throughout the rest of the schedules. The U1S
heading is not to be included in examiners' search

files, so their searches will not be affected, but industrial searchers should be able to find items more easily (51).

This heading has been applied since January 1983. It will take a few years until there is enough material in it to be really useful and, as there is no retrospective classification, the specifications classified between 1979 and 1983 will remain obscure and sometimes lost due to the confusions of the system.

U1S is arranged in three parts.

In the first part, the headings of the rest of the classification are given: thus U1S A1A is an application to do with fishing. This sets the application into context.

The second part gives uses and applications of inventions. They are divided into seven broad sequences:

Recovering and reclaiming materials
Naturally occurring and living entities
Manufactured materials technology
Energy technology
Information and control technology
Special environments

Each of these sequences devolves into lists of indexing terms.

The third part consists of utilities and properties of materials. It can be applied to only 52 of the 400-odd headings as clearly the heading must deal with an appropriate topic for properties of materials to come into it. This part of U1S is not truly universal, but as it could be applied to any heading if a property of matter were involved, it is potentially universal. As with the second part it consists of sequences of indexing terms, this time in twelve groups:

Life processes
Chemical activity
Relations with other materials
Surface properties
Flow, mechanical, weight, thermal, sound, electrical, optical and radiation properties.

There will be overlaps between schedules two and three. For instance a lubricant has lubricative properties. The more important of the two will be given but both should be searched in most cases.

Only significant items are listed: they must be mentioned in the abstract, text or examples. With multiple uses it depends how many there are. Classifiers may use their discretion.

The Catchword Index

Apart from the schedules themselves there is an index of ordinary words called "catchwords". They are arranged in alphabetical order and next to each word is an appropriate heading or choice of headings. This is the index to the classification and provides the most efficient point of entry for anyone who is not already extremely familiar with the headings.

History

The present system of sections, headings etc started in 1963. The classification itself dates back to 1852 when specifications were first printed and indexes to them were needed. Major developments began only after 1902 when examination was introduced. A detailed indexing system with a multiplicity of classes developed gradually over the years. By 1963 there were about 300 classes in 50 groups, and then the entire system was reformed. Old editions of the classifications are held with the patents they refer to, but on computerised systems the older classifications are updated so that only the most modern notation is required.

In general, one should always start with the most modern version of a classification and then search backwards checking each edition for changes. The classification will become simpler further back as less material is present.

7.2 The International Patent Classification (IPC)

This scheme was initially developed to be a unified European classification and is now used over large parts of the rest of the world as well.

A basic scheme was set up by the Council of Europe

in 1954 in the first flush of enthusiasm for European economic and industrial union. As many countries used the German patent classification or one derived from it and therefore similar, this was taken as the basic model. Development over the years was slow and the first edition was not published until 1968. Since German patent law has tended to recognise a new invention when a known development is transplanted into a new technology, the German classification was a product or industry oriented one. Therefore the first edition of the IPC was heavily product oriented.

The IPC agreement stated that members would assign and print IPC symbols on their patents whether or not this was the only classification they used. In this way searches among the patents of several countries could be carried out together. The members were still free to use their national classifications for their own patents.

The members of the IPC Union at the time of the first edition were all West European countries; the six members of the EEC and a few others. But other countries, including many non-European ones, liked the idea of unified searching and, in 1971, WIPO took over the administration of the IPC. The second edition was published in 1974, the third in 1980 and the fourth and current one in 1985 (52). A new International Convention was convened at Strasbourg to set up the IPC Union. Its objective is to make dissemination of information more efficient by serving as a search tool for both examiners and public searchers.

The first edition of the IPC was published in French and English only. Now there are many official versions in such languages as German, Russian, Japanese, Spanish, Portuguese and Czech. The non-equivalence of concepts and words in the different languages is one cause of difficulties in the use of this classification in a consistent manner.

The IPC is structured down to its very lowest levels. At the top the eight **sections** are virtually the same as those of the UK classification. When the UK version was completely redesigned in 1963, the sections were chosen with the IPC in mind.

Below the sections A-H the notation and structure are quite different. The current fourth edition will be described. Within the sections are 118 broad **classes**, which have been given numbers, and following with another letter, the **subclasses**. There are about 620 subclasses, and these are the working level of the classification, equivalent to the 400 headings in the UK classification.

Section B = performing operations, transporting
Class B64 = aircraft, aviation and cosmonautics
Subclass B64C = aeroplanes and helicopters.

The details are then contained in groups and subgroups with dots to denote hierarchy:

main group B64C 25/00 alighting gear

subgroups   B64C 25/02 . undercarriages
            25/08 . . non fixed
                      eg jettisonable
            25/10 . . . retractable, foldable
                      etc

There are approximately 7000 groups and 49000 subgroups.

Reclassification is a slow process; a new edition is produced every 5 or 6 years. This is because every country using the IPC is entitled to take part in revision sessions and each has a different view of how the classification should develop. Since the first product oriented edition, the influence of the functional tradition has turned it into a mixture: mainly function oriented terms, but application oriented where this is essential to the description of the invention. For example; F21M is the subclass for non-portable beam lighting devices or systems. Within this, F21M 3/00 covers headlights for vehicles, a very specific application, yet the technical modifications are sufficiently specific to this application to require its own classification.

Up to the third edition, the IPC had been entirely a classification. The invention was to be described as far as possible with one symbol. Another symbol could be used to classify it from a different aspect. To provide for information on anything other than the actual invention, any aspect of interest could be classified and that classification would be placed behind the symbol "//", which denotes an information unit. The information unit therefore allowed any point of interest which was not, strictly speaking, part of the invention to be noted to guide searchers. For example :

B64C 25/02 // B22C 9/00
(undercarriages // moulds or cores)

means that undercarriages are the subject of the invention and they are made in moulds or cores but this is not part of the invention.

In the fourth edition, indexing terms have been introduced for the first time, but only in a small number of classes. They are to be used to denote:

(a) essential constituents of a mixture or compound
or components of a process or structure in chemistry, or

(b) uses or applications of a classified technical subject.

Indexing terms are distinguished by having a colon between group and subgroup instead of a slash.

For example A01N 27/00 stands for pest repellants containing hydrocarbons. This will be the subject of the invention unless indicated as an information unit. A01N 27:00 codes for the same information but because it is an indexing term, the information is definitely incidental to the invention. Indexing terms are therefore very similar to information units. However, although some indexing terms can be used for classification as well, others are newly created just for indexing. In this way, informational material can be presented outside the logical framework of the classification scheme.

Full instructions are given in the schedules where indexing is to be used. Now that such terms have been introduced they will spread further with successive editions. The IPC looks deceptively simple and unstructured, but this is because of its youth. In practice it means that terms tend to be ambiguous and it is often possible to classify an item in more than one place perfectly correctly. Problems of ambiguity and lack of definition are being dealt with at each revision as tney come to attention, but, because of the continual need to compromise between national interests, it is difficult to apply solutions consistently throughout the classification.

Consistency

Problems are much more deeply rooted than can be dealt with by the revision committees. They go to the heart of the entire system. The contents of the classification is centrally controlled but in each country the terms are applied to its own specifications by its own official classifying staff or examiners. The result is that equivalent specifications, members of the same family, often end up with different symbols. The alterations can range from trivial differences between subgroups, to group differences and to differences at all levels including sections. These can arise from ambiguity regarding which terms to apply but often result from different philosophies. National criteria should not be involved when applying the IPC. However, classifications are closely linked to national patent laws and the examiners are steeped in their own laws so that their performance as classifiers is inevitably affected. To some extent wrongful application of the classification can be overcome by training and awareness but there will be an irreducible minimum variability.

Structure

Apart from the schedules, there is a catchword index serving as entry to the schedules, and a volume of summaries which lists all the sections,classes and subclasses.

There are no separate definitions given in the IPC, but brief statements are given as to what each term is classifying. In contrast, within the UK classification, at the introduction to each heading the main subject is exhaustively defined. For the IPC, the words are assumed to be understood bearing the meaning attached by daily use, the context of the schedules taking care of any multiple meanings.

Status

Twenty seven countries are members of the IPC Union and they all print IPC symbols on their specifications. Thus most countries which issue patents use the same classification at least to some extent. The international authority WIPO and the EPO, OAPI and ESARIPO use only IPC symbols for their classifications.

A number of countries, mainly European, also use the IPC as sole classification. There are over twenty including France, East and West Germany and the Netherlands. The other countries of the Union print IPC symbols but continue to use their national classification for patent office searching, construction of indexes etc. The USA and UK in particular have retained their national classifications despite playing a leading role in developing the IPC. Both these classifications have been in long use, are highly developed and (most importantly) are under national control. This means they can be revised as required and kept finely tuned to the needs of the national patent office. In these respects the IPC is at a disadvantage, particularly with the five or six year revision period which is too long for rapidly developing areas of technology. The European Patent Office develops its own interim supplements, but if these are not officially adopted, they then have problems in re-adjusting the backlog.

CAPRI − Computerised Administration of Patent documents Reclassified according to IPC

Because IPC symbols appear on most specifications they are useful in international searching systems. Therefore WIPO has set up a programme for reclssifying the entire backlog of world patents by the IPC. The first priority are those patents that comprise the PCT Minimum Documentation, but eventually all patent documents should be reclassified in this way. They will then be made into an instant patent library for those countries that wish to acquire one. It is not readily available in "developed" countries.

7.3 The US Classification

This is the oldest patent classification in use.

It is about twenty years older than the UK classification, but because its development has been continuous while the UK system started afresh in 1963, it is a much older continuous system than that of the UK.

The USC is a very simple classification to consult (53). The patents are divided broadly into three categories: chemical, electrical, and general and mechanical. These have no notation. Then there are 300 broad subject classes numbered 1 to about 350 with gaps. These deal with broad topics such as Class 5-beds. Then the classes are divided up into subclasses, as many as are needed. Subclasses are also numbered consecutively with gaps. There are about 95,000 subclasses and there is no further structure to the classification. The symbols are written out on the documents simply as

"class - subclass".

When a part of the schedule becomes full and all numbers are used, then sometimes a letter is added to denote a difference and sometimes a decimal point is introduced and further numbers included.

As with the other patent classifications, hierarchy is denoted by dots and indentations. The numbers give no indication of order.

As an example

Class 358, Pictorial communication: Television.

Subclasses

1 Natural colour television

2 . Holography

3 . Stereoscopic

4 . Recording or reproducing

5 . . Using diffraction techniques or stripe filters

6 . . Using photographic record

7 . . . With colour signal in non-pictorial form.

108

A classification symbol would be written "358 - 6" for natural colour TV using a photographic record.

The classification is determined from the most comprehensive claim. The system is almost purely function oriented and is a pure classification scheme with no indexing.

The main classification consists of one symbol chosen to fit the disclosure as closely as possible. Printed in bold type, it is followed by other symbols which may either elaborate the main classification or make cross reference to other topics. On average about four classification symbols are attached to each patent.

The US classification is a very precise one. It provides an unambiguous place for each concept. Despite being hierarchically organised and a true classification rather than an indexing scheme, the terms are not as abstract as the UK terms have become. It is in form more like the UK classification before 1979.

Structure

Apart from the schedules, there is a catchword index for entering the classification and also a manual of definitions explaining precisely what the classes and subclasses include or leave out. Being function oriented, the emphasis is on what things do rather than what they are. For instance, considering brushes, the appropriate class is

Class 15: Brushing, scrubbing, general cleaning.

Brushes then appear as implements,

```
15-159R . brushes and brooms
   159A . . . bristle configuration or composition
   ...
   190  . . tuft fasteners
   191R . . tuft socket
   194  . . . detachable tuft
   195  . . . folded tuft
   ...
```

Revision takes place continuously through the insertion of new sheets into loose leaf binders. Currently unused classification terms can be located only in a special index of obsolete classifications. When a change is made, the entire file is reclassified back to its very beginning, therefore it is only when consulting the actual patents and indexes printed at the time that the old classifications are needed.

Comparisons

We have examined the three foremost classifications in use. Ease of use depends on the type of subject matter being sought and is partly subjective.

Studies have examined the scope of different classifications in particular subject areas. The IPC is particularly slow to pick up new technology because of the long revision cycle. Under the UK system, revision takes place after the examiners report difficulties in placing particular documents, or start over-using a particular term. In the US, informal cross-disciplinary collections can be made. These form a Digest and in due course this is absorbed into the main classification (54).

7.4 International Co-operation in Classifying Patents

Each national patent office puts a vast amount of work into classifying patents. This is very time consuming and expensive and at various times offices have considered sharing the work.

The **ICIREPAT** programme was the first attempt at communal indexing of documents (55). ICIREPAT is the acronym for "International Cooperation in Information Retrieval between Examining Patent Offices". The programme was set up in the 1960s to develop a scheme for the detailed and deep indexing of particular subject areas. The indexes were intended to run first on punched cards and later on computers. The ICIREPAT members from different countries were to agree on a list of subjects and then share them out amongst themselves. Each member would do the work in one or two areas and contribute it to the entire group in return for receiving fully indexed details on all the other subjects from other group members.

For about ten years work was carried out within ICIREPAT and also independently to index small patent topics in particular ways. But the ICIREPAT venture was a failure. Different countries could not agree on which subjects should receive priority or on the emphasis of the indexing. It was also felt that the time and effort spent on indexing were not rewarded by a sufficient increase in searching effectiveness. Therefore these schemes fell generally into disuse. The UK Patent Office maintained some schemes for itself in organic chemistry and alloys in particular but with the advent of full computerisation even these will become obsolete.

ICIREPAT continued to exist and have a much more successful function in standardisation. The common layout of patent front pages, the numbering of parts of a specification for mechanical recognition and the standardised list of symbols for country names are all ICIREPAT achievements. The actual name has gone as the committee has become absorbed into WIPO and become part of PCPI (the Permanent Committee on Patent Information).

WIPO's aims in founding ICIREPAT were to ease the problems of international information retrieval on the large scale required by patent offices. There is a particular commitment to helping developing countries with small resources to set up and operate effective systems.

The administration of the international classification, IPC is a step along this road. But in order to be really useful, comprehensive IPC symbols still needed to be incorporated into a searching system. Therefore WIPO sponsored the setting up of a searching organisation in Austria. It is called **INPADOC**, the international patent documentation centre, and is a private company but with representatives of WIPO on the board. Its activities will be described in chapter 8.

7.5 Keyword Searching for Patents

Just as computer held databases have been created containing bibliographic information on journal articles, so have they been created for information on patents. Bibliographic details of patents, with or without abstracts, are searchable either in separate databases or alongside other forms of literature (56). In addition, the patents of some countries are now being held in full text in machine readable form as a consequence of being printed using computer technology. Mead Data Corporation have created a small database of full text US patents called **Lexpat**. Widespread availability of complete texts must await improved computer storage capacity, but when this is available there will be collections from a number of countries awaiting input.

To summarise, online searching of the bibliographic details and abstracts of patents is readily available and full text searching is just beginning to become available.

One set of searchable items consists of the **keywords.** Subject searching can be carried out by selecting words occurring in the text of patents. The questions being asked in patent offices are whether keyword searching is a reliable method of subject searching, and whether its adoption justifies abandoning the existing classifications (57).

Certainly for product oriented searches it seems tempting. A single search for washing machines or gas cookers could bring up all improvements whatever their nature. But one problem is that it is easy in a patent to describe a large metal enclosure with input and output pipes without ever mentioning its eventual use as a washing machine or dish washer. Different types of invention will lend themselves to various levels of use or product representations. The abstracts are intended to describe products and applications and could be a worthwhile source of keywords.

The US Patent Office is preparing to become completely paperless in its operations. As part of this, its examiners will conduct their searches on line. They have carried out extensive keyword and classification searching trials. As yet their published results are only preliminary (58). They suggest that

    (a)   keyword searching is only satisfactory when patent full text is used. Otherwise concepts are inevitably lost.

    (b)   in some areas of technology, keyword searching produced good search results but more extensive tests will be required before dispensing with the classification.

Certainly some parts of the classification will need to be retained. If any part is dispensed with, then the possibility of carrying out an effective search will depend upon the clarity of description provided by patent agents. The applicant's short term interests do not lie in allowing the document to be too easily found. One could find patent agents becoming extremely skillful at using devious, imprecise phrases which would not necessarily be easy for an examiner to detect and have rectified.

For information searchers rather than examiners, keywords and online searching remain an extremely effective means of retrieval, especially when they can be combined with use of a classification.

7.6 Indexing of Micro Organisms

The indexing, classification and searching of micro organisms involves certain special characteristics. In a patent, the organism will be mentioned by its zoological nomenclature and which itself provides sufficient indexing. Since patent classifications nowadays make provision for organisms and also for their action upon another substance, they are easily located by this means.

Under the patent laws of most countries and the International Budapest Treaty, living organisms have to be deposited in one of a number of recognised culture collections as a condition of the application proceeding and during the period a patent is in force (60). A culture collection will maintain a living sample of each organism in its care, potentially indefinitely. It provides a backup sample in case anything happens to the one in the hands of the patentee. Readers of the patent can obtain a sample for examination or for experimental purposes.

Often in the specification a culture collection number is mentioned. Organisations holding culture collections publish catalogues of their collection listing items and their availability. However these are published somewhat irregularly. They do not all give full details right down to the particular strain being cultivated, and they do not clearly give dates from when items will be available. Work by Oppenheim and Bannister(61) has indicated that patenting authorities needed to be much more aware of how organisms were being handled before licensing culture collections. See Section 5 Chapter 1 for further discussion.

Chapter 8   Patent Search Services

We have looked at the types of searches to be made. These are made available by means of a number of different services.

Searches may be carried out in order to find technical information on the state of the art or to underpin patentability or infringement arguments. They are also carried out for purposes of commercial intelligence. Retrospective searches and also current awareness searches may be required for any type of application. The techniques of searching tend to be the same irrespective of purpose, so that the descriptions will concentrate on retrospective searching and indicate current awareness aspects as we go along.

8.1 Patent Office and Library Services

In Britain, most of the services normally provided by a patent office library are provided by the Science Reference Library which used to be the Patent Office library and is housed in the original Patent Office building just off Chancery Lane, London. It has recently been renamed tne Science Reference and Information Service, SRIS. The Patent Office and library services are interlinked and were provided in the same building until recently.The Patent Office has now moved a short distance to State House in High Holborn, London but may have to move on again in 1987.The SRIS is scheduled to move as part of the British Library to its new St Pancras building in the 1990s. Many SRIS services are reproduced in a number of selected libraries around the country (The Patents Information Network). We will describe the SRIS services first and list other libraries at the end.

The indexes available in the SRIS are strictly unofficial, the Patent Office takes no responsibility for faulty indexing or patents missed out of searches (62).

8.1.1 Name indexes

The Patent Office publishes an Official Journal for its patent work. It appears weekly and is called OJ(P) to distinguish it from the OJ for trade marks. In the OJ(P) appear bibliographic details of initial applications and these details are repeated when the applications are published. In both cases there is a name index of applicants. The OJ(P) is available weekly in the SRIS but is never collated and is therefore useful for current awareness work only.

A name index on cards of all applicants is held for six years in the SRIS. This collates names with application numbers only and is destroyed after the six years.

A name index of applicants and also of inventors is compiled on computer and is available in weekly runs collated quarterly in the SRIS. Each year's collection is bound up in a volume and the run of names back to the earliest printed specifications is available in the SRIS. Inventors' names have not always been made available and even now are not compulsory, therefore this is best regarded as an index of applicants and patentees. Prior to 1979 it was bound up every 25,000 specifications, since then collation is annual.

When a company has patents listed, the name of the inventor, or first inventor, will be included next to each patent number. This is very useful when a large company is being sought. It is regrettable that inventors' names are not systematically available as they are always given to the Patent Office itself.

Name indexes for European and PCT documents are also available.

8.1.2 Legal status information

The Patent Office maintains the official Register

of Patents. The patents are listed in numerical order of the published specifications. Dates of application, publication and grant are given as are the name and address of the patentee. Dates of lapse or expiry of the patent are listed if these have occurred. If legal proceedings are taken, these are noted with their results. Licences should also be included but this is not always the case and the penalty for not doing so is only a small fine.

To consult the Register an enquirer has to pay a fee for each patent of interest, currently £2.00. For this, he can consult the Register and also the file wrapper, the official file on that application or patent. The Register and file can be consulted on the Patent Office premises only, but certified photocopies can be made of the documents for a fee.

In the SRIS are unofficial registers compiled each week from the OJ(P). One is an application register relating application numbers to publication numbers. The other is a register of stages of progress. Applications are listed by publication number and date of first publication and second publication or withdrawal are noted. A date of lapse or expiry is also given.

For PCT documents there is only an applications register available at the SRIS. PCT applications then enter national systems and there are no more separate registers. For the European applications, the register can be consulted by computer link to the EPO from the SRIS. This consultation is carried out by the library staff, who will do it very quickly and efficiently. Alternatively, the EPO register is available to any searcher who can connect via the telephone system and a computer terminal to the international data network. The actual files are available at the EPO in Munich but can be ordered by post to be consulted in the patent offices of any member state. These files will contain photocopies so that the original remains with the EPO. The files and register are officially correct documents. The SRIS also holds printed indexes relating to granted European patents designating the UK and a list in numerical order of dates when the A and B specifications of all European patents were received in the library. This last index is unofficial, but the separate list of UK designations is official, being sent from the EPO.

INPADOC provides legal status information for six countries from Vienna online or on microfiche, updated weekly. It obtains this information by virtue of the special relationship with patent offices which stems from its WIPO link. Details of INPADOC's operations generally are given later in this chapter.

Patent families

These are not available from national patent offices as they deal with national applications only. Family indexes were introduced by the multi-country specialist patent databases.

Patent specifications

Once a week the newly published British, European, and PCT documents are laid out in the SRIS public reading room for one week. Searchers can look through them one by one for current awareness purposes. All three sequences are numbered in classification order each week so that searchers can brouse in appropriate subject areas.

For British applications, the front pages are also published separately from the full specification and are collected together as a searching tool. They will be considered in the next section.

8.1.3 Subject indexes

Each week in the Official Journal, a rudimentary subject index is published, listing patent numbers under assigned headings of the British patent classification. The weekly subject index is also published separately, to be filed alongside the abstracts. Patent numbers are listed against every complete classification mark noted on the patents. When the abstracts are bound, they are divided into 25 groups of headings. The relevant part of the classification, and the subject index, are included in each volume. Therefore when searching back through a number of volumes, it is easy to check whether or not the classification has changed.

The 1949 Act abridgments are organised in the same

way as the abstracts, with the appropriate
classification and subject index in each volume.

The Patent Office also offers a batch-mode
computer search. These are called "file lists"
because they correspond to the contents of the
examiners' files. These may be requested for one
classification mark only or for a number combined
via Boolean logic. The series cover different time
spans. Single term file lists from 1911 to 1965
(patent number 1 000 000) are available in printed
form in the SRIS. These are series A. The most
important series is labelled D, multi term file
lists from Number 1 000 000 to the present. Up to
100 terms are allowed. This seems a vast number
but might be needed when specifying complex
chemical compounds or alloys. Series B consists of
single terms in patents from Number 1 000 000 to
the present. Series C has been discontinued.

File lists are ordered by filling in a form and
paying a fee. The present-day classification is
used and the computer takes account of all changes
as it searches backwards. One must determine the
classifications to be used from the schedules and
try them out manually on the abstracts and
abridgments. The computer produces a list of
patent numbers, eliminating any duplication of
numbers which appear under different
classification terms. The normal procedure is to
look up the abstracts or abridgments and to
consult the actual patent specification only when
satisfied as to relevance in any given search.
There are unlikely to be a large number of
directly relevant specifications.

File lists can also be used for current awareness
purposes. One can establish a file list request as
a recurrent weekly SDI service and receive either
a list of numbers or copies of specifications as
they appear.

A crucial part of the subject searching facilities
provided for patents are the volumes of
classification schedules. For most systematic
searching, one needs the most recent volume only.
For each heading, applicability for file lists is
explained.

Sometimes a file is closed. This happened
particularly often at the classification revision

in 1979. This means that revisions are not back-dated past that point and neither are term frequencies.

Computerisation

The Rayner Commission on Civil Service efficiency recommended that the Patent Office buy its own computer. It is now planning to do so. A number of the more clerical parts of Patent Office services will be computerised, and the classification and information retrieval services will be included in the scheme. Once they have been made available to Patent Office staff they will also be open to public use. Charging and availability have not yet been decided.

The first services to be computerised will be those connected with the Trade Marks Registry (see Section 4, Chapter 4). Progress is fairly slow and publicly available services are not scheduled before the next decade. Hiving off the Patent Office might change this time scale.

The Patent Information Network

Patents used to be held in large numbers of libraries, but due to low levels of use, access has been concentrated onto a relatively small number of public libraries in large towns. The SRIS acts as co ordinator of a network of such libraries. **Provincial patent libraries** hold stocks of actual patent documents plus related journals and indexes. There are eight of them and the countries they hold in stock are varied depending on local demand. The libraries concerned are those of Belfast, Birmingham, Glasgow, Leeds, Liverpool, Manchester, Newcastle-Upon-Tyne and Sheffield. **Patent information centres** hold UK abridgments and abstracts and a number of patent journals. There are eighteen of these (63).

8.2 Commercial Services

Technical journals. Many periodicals list new patents for current awareness and information purposes. These will fall within the interests covered by that journal but there is unlikely to be a comprehensive and coherent collection policy and there may be considerable delay between publication and reporting. Therefore this is not a useful source for systematic searching.

8.2.1 Standard abstracting services

Many working scientists and engineers consult abstracting services as a matter of course as do information scientists. Some cover patents along with other forms of literature but one must be aware that often the coverage is patchy and some do not cover patents at all. There are also specialist services which cover patents only. These will be described under a separate heading.

The chemical sciences seem traditionally to be the most ready to use patents as information sources. Chemical Abstracts has a wide coverage intended to be comprehensive at least in major countries. In a survey of coverage of British patents carried out by Mann and Hellyer (64), Chemical Abstracts was found to have left out two patents which described new chemicals, so it is not entirely reliable. It also does not fully cover foreign language patents from countries which may be prolific producers but speak a minority language such as Belgium, the Netherlands, Japan and the USSR. Apart from Chemical Abstracts, good coverage in both chemical and non-chemical areas is given mainly by specialised journals concentrating on small subject areas. These include World Aluminium Abstracts, Zinc Abstracts and Plastics Abstracts. In the case of any one journal one must check the policy and scope of coverage before using it.

Quite a number of journals do not cover patents at all, for instance Physics Abstracts. Often this is due to the immense quantity of literature much of which is of little use and often repetitive. However, it has been shown in a number of narrow, well defined subject areas that coverage of about 75% of all patents can be obtained by scanning only four or five countries. These have to be determined for each subject area. They will be the countries in which the inventions are most likely to be exploited and which are used either as priority patenting countries or in which many patentees take out equivalents (65).

Quite a number of the publishers of abstracting journals mount the same information on a computer to form a database and one is able to undertake online patent searching via this route using bibliographical details and an abstract. With patents, one can search on a number of characteristics different from those of journal references : numbers, dates and classifications being major examples. The process of online searching is, however, the same. Since the value of an online file lies in particular in its completeness and in its backlog, these files are of strictly limited usefulness.

A particularly useful file is that of Chemical Abstracts because for each patent mentioned, a list of equivalents is also provided.

8.2.2 Specialist patent services

These are commercial services devoted entirely to patents and cover either one or a number of countries. They are all mounted as online services and most have associated printed services as well.

The services to be described are:
> Patsearch,
> Claims,
> INPI,
> INPADOC, and
> Derwent.

Patsearch
This is an online file of US and PCT patents mounted on the British host, Pergamon Infoline.

The US file contains all the information on US front pages from 1970 onwards. This includes titles, abstracts, priority details, numbers, names and examiners' citations. Since 1984 the main claim has also been included. All components are searchable fields and individual words are searchable from the title, abstract and claim.

The PCT file goes back to the start of publication in 1979 and contains abstracts, bibliographic information and search reports which are at the back rather than on the front page. It is a true report rather than a mere list of citations because it includes additional information : the number of any claim affected by a citation or an indication that a citation was made for background information only.

One piece of information often found on front pages but lacking on online systems is the drawing. The telephone lines can transmit enough definition to enable drawings to be included, but the process would be unreasonably slow. It would take 5-10 minutes to transmit one drawing and as the terminal would be needed to remain connected to the network, this would become rather too expensive to be practical. Drawings are valuable because often an abstract will refer to the drawing or perhaps a chemical formula diagram. In such cases a searcher derives little benefit from the text alone. To overcome this, Infoline introduced "Videopatsearch". Subscribers received a videodisc player and eight discs each the size of an LP to cover the twelve years 1970 to 1982. The player was plugged into the online terminal and when a search had been carried out and the correct disc put on, a command from the terminal would locate the drawing corresponding to a document number. One had to remain online while viewing the drawing: two screens were provided so that text and drawing could be examined simultaneously. It was possible to print out drawings from the terminal. The subscription was expensive and the equipment was cumbersome and expensive to use. This was an idea ahead of its time and was quietly dropped when the clients remained away. It is likely that an improved version will be introduced in due course.

Patsearch covers only patents from the USA and PCT. Other countries are to be added in due course but in separate files. Pergamon has signed a contract with the British Patent Office and will have a British patents file up sometime in late 1986 or early 1987. Although the machine-readable data is taken from the Patent Office, this file is quite separate from the in-house file being created by the Office. When that becomes available to the public, the two services will compete.

Claims is also an online file of US patents. It is mounted on Dialog, the largest US online host system and also on SDC. The US Patent Office has leased its patent file to a number of hosts. Claims is of particular interest because it has the most extensive backlog extending to 1950. This backlog applies to chemical patents only. All other patents, ie electrical and mechanical, are covered from 1963 onwards. Reissues and defensive publications started in 1971. Design patents, which correspond to registered designs in the UK, started in 1980. The Dialog file is split into several chronological segments. For current awareness there is a weekly file of the last six weeks. There are also a number of associated files : deep indexing for chemical patents and a register of chemical compounds, US classification codes and a file of the examiners' citations listed on the front pages of US patents. Abstracts are available from 1971 onwards and the most comprehensive claim from 1965. The Claims files are not widely accessed in the UK but are overall well used.

INPI is a set of online files mounted by the French Patent Office on Telesystemes-Questel. There are four files. The first contains details of all French patent specifications published since 1969 and the second covers all European patents. Information on other family members and an index in IPC order to all these patents comprise the other two files. As with Claims, this service is valuable but not much used in the UK because of duplication by other services.

8.2.3 INPADOC

This is a multi-country system covering 55 authorities, the widest coverage of any database (66). The organisation, "International Patent Documentation Centre" is based in Vienna. It is a private company set up by the Austrian Government in association with WIPO. Any patent issuing authority can become a member. The members send their weekly or monthly records of published documents to Vienna. These are entered onto a computer without any additions or modifications. The output is then the computer database plus a series of indexes printed on COM microfiche straight from the computer. Patent offices of member states have access to all the output. Other organisations can subscribe to it. Members joined at different times but most records go back to 1968. One must check the starting date for each country if in doubt. These are given as part of the main documentation of the system.

The database consists of purely bibliographical details, there are no abstracts. Titles are in the language of the specification, transliterated where necessary. The rest of the information consists of numbers, dates, countries and names all in standardised format and order.

The computer file and COM indexes are updated weekly. The indexes produced each week arrange the patents as follows:
    in IPC order,
    in applicant/patentee order,
    in inventor order,
    in numerical order for each country, and
    giving all previous family members.

The weekly collection is published together as a patent gazette. Quarterly cumulations of each index are published separately. Annual and 5 yearly cumulations are also produced.

Because of the agreement with WIPO, each member patent office must make all the indexes freely available for public access except the family index. This one is to be charged for as INPADOC is a private company and must make a profit to survive. Pergamon markets the fiche and database in W.Europe and the USA. A variety of agreements for free distribution and for marketing exist in other parts of the world.

The online database is available by a direct telephone link with Vienna. For British users it is most conveniently mounted on Infoline alongside the Patsearch database already described. It is the largest database on Infoline and is all held in one file. There is also a separate file of the most recent 15 weeks called "Inpanew". There are no stopwords; any word can be searched because of the diversity of languages and vocabularies. However, titles are notoriously uninformative and in practice it is usually more useful to search for names, dates and numbers.

Family searching is carried out by searching for patents with the same priority data. The algorithm for this special search is recursive so that, when all direct members of the family have been found (first cousins), it checks whether any of these have a second (or further) priority date and finds all members of that family thus building up cousins of all orders.

It is intended by Infoline to install a cross-file

searching facility so that if a US or PCT patent is found via INPADOC, its abstract can be read in Patsearch.

Another possible abstract is that on Chemical Abstracts. Infoline puts the CA abstract number into the records of chemical patents as a further cross reference. It is not a searchable term but is displayed. Chemical Abstracts is not available on Infoline but can be consulted elsewhere once the abstract number is known.

Statistical analysis

A special Infoline command "Get" is available for creating time series and rankings. When a set of patents has been created after a search, then a ranked list of, for instance, IPC subclasses or of industrial companies which are patentees can be created. Ranked lists of any searchable field can be displayed. Evolution over time is another informative characteristic and is also available using "Get" (67).

Legal status information for eight countries is held on a separate file of INPADOC data and is also available on microfiche (68). The computer version is available only from Vienna. The fiche are now freely available in the SRIS.

Another entirely separate file is **CAPRI**, patent documents reclassified by IPC. The coverage stretches from 1975 backwards covering the PCT minimum documentation countries and eventually all others. Each country will work backwards until all its patents are covered. This service is neither generally available nor of interest in Western Europe. It is intended for developing countries where it can be used to create an instant library of patent documents for a newly created patent office or central scientific library.

8.2.4 Derwent Publications Ltd

Derwent and INPADOC are the two big multi-country services and are natural rivals.

Some of Derwent's services are much older than those of INPADOC. Others are more recent. The main differences are that Derwent covers only 32 sources (to INPADOC's 55). These consist of 28 countries plus the EPO and WIPO-PCT and also two defensive publication journals: Research Disclosures and International Technological Disclosures. Derwent creates its own input; all titles, abstracts and indexing terms are written by Derwent's own staff to a reliable standard oriented to the needs of the industrial clients (69). Defensive publications journals publish disclosures of technical ideas (paid for by the column inch) with the intention of getting them into the prior art so that no one else can patent them. The journals are sent free of charge to all patent offices.

A certain amount of history is essential for a full understanding of the particular services available. There are now so many that it is unclear how they are related, and why those particular services were mounted in the first place.

To start with, Derwent deals mainly with patent literature. The few non-patent journals produced are irrelevant here and will not be mentioned further. It is a private company now wholly owned by International Thomson Plc.

Derwent was founded in 1951 by Monty Hyams, a chemist. He published abstracts journals covering all the published patents of a number of countries, in particular Belgium.

Belgium was particularly important as it grants patents by a registration system after a brief formalities check. They are not actually published, but one copy of the document is made available to the public in the Patent Office in Brussels within a few weeks of the application. No published applications were available at this time so that patents in other countries were published only after several years of examination. Therefore the Belgian patents were a unique source of rapid information, and Derwent publications soon established a high reputation as being an accessible guide to these documents. Single country bulletins are still produced for six countries.

In 1963 Mr Hyams started Central Patents Index, now called Chemical Patents Index, with a large investment from a group of pharmaceutical companies to develop sophisticated chemical searching services for them. CPI started with pharmaceuticals, then progressed to agricultural chemicals, and then to other chemicals. It covers a large number of countries providing not only titles, abstracts and a rough classification scheme, but also complex chemical coding designed for searching chemical structures. Subscribers to these services are charged a high subscription fee and then pay for the specific services used. For this they receive highly "value added" information. Thus the large pharmaceutical and chemical industries developed a symbiotic relationship with Derwent. The published journals available to non-subscribers as well did not contain the structural indexes. This distinction between subscriber and non- subscriber services was carried over to the online services when they started.

In 1974 World Patents Index was started. This covered all the non-chemical patents missed by CPI but without any sophisticated indexing.

In 1976 the combined file of CPI and WPI was marketed as an online service with an integrated file called WPI. This was mounted exclusively by System Development Corporation, SDC, using the Orbit searching language. WPI is a bibliographic file only. Abstracts were introduced in 1981 when the WPI file was closed and a second one, WPIL ("WPI Latest") was opened.

To summarise, parts of the WPI file, those covering pharmaceuticals, extend back to 1963. Other parts were introduced in phases, the latest date being 1974.

Derwent files are no longer exclusive to SDC and are available on a number of hosts including Dialog and Telesystemes. However, SDC has recently been taken over by Pergamon-Infoline and this implies a partial merger of the two multi-country services, at least in their on line forms.

The current organisation of Derwent's operations is as follows. When a new patent comes in, the file is checked to see that it is not an equivalent of a patent already dealt with. If it is, then it is given the accession number of the basic and dealt with no further. If not, then it is sent to a specialist to have a title, abstract and indexing terms added. When ready, the text is typed into the computer. Two magnetic tapes are made, one for the online file and one to drive the printer. This will print out the abstract and bibliographic details in any configuration required to produce a number of specialised journals or indexes: alerting bulletins, weekly lists of new basics over a wide range of subjects or monthly lists of all patents in a narrow subject area. The sources are not all covered equally. There are major countries where all patents are included, and minor ones where only patents with equivalents in one or more major countries are covered.

Other Services

Electrical patents index

This is a deep indexing system aiming to do for the electrical and electronics industry what CPI did for the chemical. It started in 1981 and pays its way.

US files

Derwent have mounted the US patent files from 1971 onwards. These files offer the same material as the US part of Patsearch, viz. the front page information.

The workstation

Derwent have developed a package for statistical manipulation. Unlike the Inpadoc version it does not run on the main host computer. The results of a search must be downloaded to a micro computer and can then be manipulated with special software called "Patstat". The statistics it produces are the same as those obtainable using Inpadoc but, having a micro computer avoids the online connect time and is therefore cheaper to use. Like the rest of the system, this part is designed for high power large scale use. In contrast Inpadoc is best used on a small scale (70).

Family searching

As mentioned, members of a family in WPI are given the same accession number. Therefore family searching implies searching for all patents with the same accession number. A patent with more than one priority will have additional accession numbers and there is no relationship between numbers with which to trace relationships. This system finds only the immediate family, the first cousins, not more distant relations, although a recursive programme could be written to do so. In this respect the software is inferior to that used with Inpadoc. It is also clumsy in that each time an equivalent is published, the WPI file must be opened to add it. With Infoline files, new patents are added serially as they occur.

New technology

Derwent, being a very large concern, is in a good position to experiment with new technology. As new storage media and computing techniques come on the market, Derwent is among the first to try them out. It also funds research into computer handling of chemical structures and takes a general interest in progress in information science.

In general, Derwent services are highly sophisticated and are tailored to the needs of large industry, primarily the chemical and the electrical. It remains popular partly by being very responsive to its users. Every year subscribers' meetings are held where new Derwent plans are unveiled and customers' comments on old and new services are listened to. Costs are estimated and if enough customers are interested, Derwent staff are willing to put on any service requested.

8.3 Sources of Patent Law

Concentrating on the United Kingdom, a patent is defined and circumscribed in law by the **Patents Act 1977**. This is published and made available, as are all Acts of Parliament, by HMSO. Some of the finer details of practice were left to the Patent Office to organise and these are published in a volume of **Patent Rules** first issued in 1978 and revised in 1982. The Rules cover practical details such as the precise content and layout of the

forms which are to be filled in. When the Rules
are amended they are laid before Parliament but
not debated unless a Member feels this to be
necessary.

Apart from the Statute, precise interpretation of
the law in specific instances is enshrined in case
law which takes effect through the system of
precedents. Patent cases are civil actions and
take place in the High Court. A participant has
automatic right of appeal to the Court of Appeal
disputing either the facts or the law. If the
issue at stake is certified to be a point of law
of major public importance the appeal can go one
stage further to the House of Lords which is the
highest Court in the land. At each level of the
hierarchy, judges must follow precedents from
courts higher than or equal to themselves. Thus
the Court of Appeal is bound by itself and by the
House of Lords. It can over-rule the High Court
but judges there are bound to follow the latest
ruling from the Court of Appeal. A precedent is
binding if the facts of an earlier case are such
that the essential point of law to be decided is
the same as that of the earlier case. A lawyer's
skill is to select the precedents required to
steer the judgment in the desired direction. The
House of Lords normally follows its earlier
decisions for the sake of consistency. It
does,however, reserve the right to change its mind
when it feels this to be necessary in order to
respond to a change in perception of particular
needs or facts, or when it feels that an earlier
decision was in error.

This system of precedents is a fine and flexible
tool of lawmaking. It depends entirely upon
effective reporting of cases and their easy
retrieval.

Before a case gets to court it will normally have
had a hearing in the Patent Office which itself
acts judicially. The transcripts of these cases
appear in the Science Reference Library under the
title "Patent,Trade Mark and Design Decisions".
They are not published but, as they have no
precedent rating, they are less valuable anyway.

Court decisions appear in volumes of law reports.
Some of wider interest might appear in a set of
general reports which are published weekly:

The Weekly Law Reports,
The Law Reports (Chancery Division),
The All England Law Reports, and
Appeal Cases.

There are two specialist series dealing with all forms of intellectual property:
Reports of Patent,Trade Mark and Design Cases (RPCs), and
Fleet Street Reports (FSRs).
These are published monthly and have a broadly similar coverage. The RPCs are published by statute and are the only official law reports in the country.

EEC cases appear in The European Law Reports, and Common Market Law Reports.

For current awareness, a case guide appears in the European Intellectual Property Review, EIPR, and Intellectual Property Decisions, a current awareness journal.

Many new books and journals are appearing in this field as it generates much interest.

Online legal systems

Butterworths' **Lexis** is the predominant online legal database in the UK. It carries general law and intellectual property law files for Britain and the USA and gradually hopes to extend to other countries (71). It has the reputation of being a cumbersome system to use in that it requires one to possess a dedicated terminal. This does have the advantage that special keys and functions can be programmed into it. However, protests from potential users at the expense and inconvenience have pursuaded Mead Data Central (its developer and owner in America) to approve a limited number of ordinary micro computers for use as Lexis terminals. With careful planning it is possible to integrate Lexis use with other uses of the terminal and to standardise on one system.

All marketing efforts are aimed at large groups of lawyers with high use levels. Butterworths do not believe their system is suitable for non-lawyers and are not particularly interested in involving information specialists or any type of small occasional users. Because of this, becoming acquainted with the system is somewhat difficult. However, once acquired, familiarity with Lexis does allow effective searching of what is in its files.

Lawtel, a small viewdata system, is useful mainly for current awareness (72). It operates as a closed user group entered through Prestel and it covers both recent cases and the progress of legislation through Parliament. Using a tie-in to Lexis, a searcher who finds a recent case reference on Lawtel can view the transcript once mounted on the Lexis computer. The transcript is usually available much sooner than a law report and many cases are not reported at all.

In the **USA** a leading journal of cases and administrative decisions is **US Patent Quarterly**. The printed journal is available from the publishers in the usual way but the bibliographical details and headnotes (abstracts), are available as a file called **Patlaw** on Infoline.

Chapter 9   The Value of Patent Information

Having seen what patent documents are and how to search the literature, we must now investigate the characteristics of the literature and the uses to which its contents can be put.

9.1 Characteristics of the Literature

Much information disclosed in a patent specification is unique. If not unique, the patent is usually the earliest publication and will contain more detailed information than any other documentation (73).

Uniqueness

A number of studies have examined further publications of material that has appeared in a patent. The earliest studies merely searched for the names of patentees and of inventors in a number of relevant abstracting services and some primary journals to find papers they may have written covering the subject matter of the patent.

Using this method, in 1974 Liebesny (74) found that only about 6% of British patents are associated with corresponding publications elsewhere. Allen and Oppenheim (75) found 11% and 6% for Canadian and US patents respectively (75). These studies looked at samples over the entire range of patent subjects. They found a spread over broad subject areas with chemical patents resulting in far more additional publications, 15-20% and electrical and general and mechanical patents far fewer, 3-10%. A number of single subject studies were also carried out in the same way producing comparable figures; patents for animal feedstuffs had an overlap of 20% with the journal literature for instance (76). This figure is at the top end of the range.This is probably due to more specialised abstracts journals being searched which uncovered additional publications.

However, these are all lower limits rather than correct estimates of coverage because people other than the named inventors could have written about an invention. Other potential authors might be associates of the inventors or participants at a later stage of development such as product design. Even the name of the patentee (if it is a company) may not be useful if a firm wishes to avoid publicity apart from its own commercial efforts. Therefore a more accurate measure would involve subject searching as well as name searching for articles.

Such a study was carried out by OTAF, the US Department of Commerce, Office of Technological Assessment and Forecasting(77). They examined two samples of US patents published in 1967 and 1972. Name searches were carried out for all patents and extensive subject searches for a sample. Overall it was found that where name searches related 10.5% of patents to articles, the subject searches raised this to 16%. Only substantial disclosure in an article of the content of the patent document was counted.

An interesting contrast is to be drawn where the material disclosed is not of commercial interest. There are many patents which describe medically important antibiotics released by micro organisms into their surrounding culture medium. The patent gives a detailed description of the organism but the commercial interest centres on the antibiotic. Two investigations have looked at descriptions of the taxonomy of these organisms in microbiological journals and found 20-40% disclosures depending on the organisms (78). 40% is very high in comparison with the earlier figures and indicates the non-commercial nature of the information. But results ranging over 20% also indicate such variability and uncertainty as to make more detailed predictions valueless.

Patent groups

The works just described portray a rather low
recapitulation of patented results in other media.
However, there is no attempt to distinguish
important work from that which is less useful. In
two separate projects (79), students looked for
groups of patents of one company, or centred on a
key inventor (who may have changed company), which
delineated a single project. It was found that in
the two fields of pharmaceuticals and of food
preparation about half the patents fell into
groups. Associated publications for a group could
then be interpreted much more generously than for
a single patent as anything which discussed the
research programme, its motivation or its results.
In this way average overlap rates of 60% for the
pharmaceutical patents and 26% for the food
preparation patents were found. Considering the
structure of these two industries the disparity in
results is not unexpected. Both are relatively
high figures and indicate a healthy interchange of
information between patent "authors" and the
producers of the main body of scientific and
technical literature.

Currency

Patent specifications are often published earlier
than journal articles. The studies which first
demonstrated the low overlap also showed that the
peak of journal publications occurs two years
after publication of the specification. These
figures related to traditional systems where the
specification would have been examined and
accepted by the Patent Office before publication.
In countries where the unexamined application is
published, another one to two years need to be
added to the difference with respect to journal
articles. Such a lag is bound to occur as the
patent disclosure must be prepared in advance of
any other.

Longer delays can be caused by commercial
considerations. A company may not allow
publication of details until the product is fully
developed. The details have to be disclosed in a
patent but it is likely that comparatively few
people will read this. A journal article is likely
to attract far more attention. A case study was
made of "Galvalume" a waterproof coating for

roofs. A number of patents were published, but no articles or trade literature were produced for seven years. Then one article appeared giving only scanty details. This was an invention which aroused great interest. Of the many searchers on its trail, someone would have found other accessible descriptions had there been any (80).

Other Characterstics

Patent literature is relatively inaccessible in public collections. Patents tend to be kept together and apart from other technical literature in specially designated libraries. In Britain there are only seven public libraries holding patent documents, and only the SRIS has extensive collections of foreign patents. There are other libraries holding patent indexes and abstracts but even these are few and far between.

Some companies will maintain their own collections, but this is unusual as it is difficult, costly, time and space consuming to collect patents comprehensively, even in a fairly narrow subject range.This is mainly due to duplication of documents within one system and over a number of countries. The latter is somewhat reduced by the increasing popularity of regional systems and of the PCT route.

A study carried out in Newcastle-Upon-Tyne demonstrated that if ordinary small and medium sized local industries are given adequate instruction in the use of patents, they soon see their value. Demand on the Newcastle public library patent services has grown. New users continued to require access after the experiment had finished, demonstrating that their interests were genuine and not just artifacts of the experiment (81). A study reported recently in Liverpool confirms that widespread ignorance is the main barrier to the use of patents (82).

Another barrier is the language in which patents are written, the rather obscure "patentese", a technical language constructed to be simultaneously broad and yet precise enough to satisfy the legal requirements of patent disclosure without circumscribing the invention or giving away more information than is required. This is no genuine barrier to communication as

motivation to read the document and familiarity
with the technical terms encourages adjustment to
the clumsy wording.

A far more serious reason for technical staff not
to refer to patent literature is that, contrary to
law, the literature often does not stand alone and
allow the reader to replicate the invention. There
are always further details to be refined such as
making a choice of materials or finding a reaction
temperature to use out of a range. UK law says
that the best method must be disclosed but it does
not have to be labelled as such, it can be hidden
among many. The only exception is that the most
suitable chemical formula must be given in the
abstract for that patent. It may sometimes be the
case that various possibilities are given because
a patent has been applied for so early in the
product's lifetime that the inventor has not yet
identified which components work best together.
Taken to extremes this is an abuse of the patent
system. The examiners should insist on greater
clarity and explicitness; but, without practical
experience of the invention it is difficult for
them to identify points of serious ambiguity or to
tell what information is likely to be genuinely
ambiguous or where the applicant is being
deliberately obscure.

It is normal practice that, when an agreement to
license a patented invention is concluded, there
will be a "know how" agreement as well. Know how
is the detailed knowledge of exactly what to do to
incorporate the invention into a commercially
produced and saleable product. Much of this will
be of commercial rather than technical value, and
may consist of very simple non-inventive matter,
but the importance attached to know how is so
great that its absence from the published patent
is somewhat to be regretted. It would be an
interesting experiment for a referee to examine
know how agreements involving patented inventions
for useful material and to require this material
to be appended to the patent. In this way,
developments made after the patent was applied for
would not be lost to the public domain.

9.2 Technical and Commercial Applications

A. Technical information

This will be obtained from a subject search covering one or a number of countries perhaps backed up with name searches among known workers in a field. There are several uses for the information found.

a) **Solving technical problems**
   Before the start of any research and development project it is advisable to examine the patent literature. The same problem may have been encountered either in the same or analogous technology in the past, and either solutions were found or at least non-productive avenues revealed. Such a search may obviate the need for this R&D project all together. If work goes ahead then current awareness searching should pick up work being presently undertaken.

b) **Accessories to a main product**
   A company may successfully manufacture a product and then need to install accessories either ready made or requiring mastery of subsidiary technologies. Patent searching here would concentrate on current awareness to obtain the latest improvements. For instance a lorry manufacturer needs to know about loading ramps, hubcaps for the tyres, a retractable sunroof for the cab, improved headlights and a multitude of other products.

c) **New products**
   Many successful companies have to face great competition in their established products and therefore try to diversify their activities into a range of related products. Their current expertise will dictate a range of options for other products and technologies. A patent search among other things, could reveal potential products. The name and address of the patentee are given and discussions on exploitation could then follow.

B. Techno-commercial information

This is a form of commercial intelligence, using

the literature to predict corporate plans and new products. The basis for such work is to collect all the patents published by one firm or within one technology and group of firms in a particular time span and then analyse their contents (83).

The patents of one firm

From the patent portfolio of a firm one can see what product or technology is being worked on and what problems are being tackled. Solutions to these problems can result in either an improved product or a new one. The patents will give advanced warning of likely products and other firms can angle their advertising or improve their technologies accordingly. A strong advertising campaign can do much to change attitudes to technology. For example, Japanese TV companies made small screen TV sets popular via advertising. Until then all assumed that bigger sets were better and angled their advertising accordingly.

Active inventors within a firm can be identified. One or two names will crop up in conjunction with different colleagues on a series of patents and these will be the key people with ideas whose activities would be worth watching. It may be possible to recruit them for your own firm or at least to follow their careers.

Finally, the patent portfolio denotes the health of a company. It indicates the existence or non-existence of a continuing successful research effort. This is useful information for anyone interested in a company whether as a job applicant or in preparation for a takeover or anything in between.

The patents of a group of firms

Patents can indicate the technical trends and health of an entire industry.

For national firms, important information is the number of new applications and whether they are rising or falling. It indicates whether activity in a field is growing, mature or declining, and also shows which firms are most active and which individuals within firms are creating most of the technology. Internationally one can see which countries are active in which technologies.

In statistical analyses based on journal articles, the finest details are obtained by counting the citations authors make to articles. With patents one can count the citations made by examiners to other patents. They are not made for the same purpose as journal citations and yet the effect is similar, to give an interlocking network of related documents which cite each other and define a subject area. This technique will show research fronts and also the closest competitors for specific lines of research.

Patent statistical studies

The study of patent statistics is the discipline underlying techno-commercial analyses. Such statistics are normally gathered from patent front pages and search reports. They can be used to pinpoint growth points in the technology and identify rival firms. Productivity can be determined at the level of laboratories, firms, whole industries and countries (84).

The Swiss watch industry was devastated when digital watches were introduced despite a long warning period from patent specifications. Since then a patent information centre has been set up, financed by the industry to keep them better informed (85).

The statistical packages offered by Derwent and by Pergamon-Infoline allow any firm to carry out its own in-house statistical analyses. Large companies are very interested in doing this. Until these facilities were introduced such work was only carried out on one or two dedicated databases covering mainly US patents.

Computer Horizons is a large private US company with a database of US patents. It carries out consultancy work for firms and also for government departments based upon patent statistics as well as other sources.

OTAF which belonged to the US Department of Commerce used to conduct surveys of particular industries and the place of the US in the world's industrial effort. Every year it published a report of these studies. It also did consultancy work. Its database was the US Patent Office's computerised files. OTAF was a very highly respected organisation and produced some valuable work. Unfortunately it was closed down in one of the Reagan administration's budget cutting exercises. Its work has not ceased entirely as some functions have been taken over by another Department of Commerce body. This is the OTA, Office of Technical Assessment, which does a lot of commercial forecasting but using economic indicators mainly. To some extent the abolition of OTAF is more in the nature of a merger with OTA.

The work of these organisations was carried out almost exclusively by way of US analyses because their databases consist of US documents plus a number of equivalents. They were the pioneers of this type of work and the only two organisations which offered a continuous patent monitoring exercise. Computer Horizons continues its services but nowadays the online systems are providing very effective competition.

For European countries, the EEC Commission has published some statistical analyses as a one-off exercise (86). So has the OECD. In Britain, the Science Policy Research Unit at Sussex University and the Technical Change Centre in London have carried out a number of discrete patent based analyses as part of a wider programme of examining scientific advances and their effects on technology and on society.

The programme of patent studies at The City University, London, is an example of the contribution of academic departments to a whole range of investigations (87). The details of how a scheme works and how it varies from subject to subject are carried out in series of small studies which cumulate over the years to produce a worthwhile compendium of information. Commercial organisations do not have the time for this sort of work and even governmental bodies need a reason for each group they study.

9.3 Legal-commercial Information

The technical and techno-commercial uses of patent information represent the true value of the system to industry. However, to a great extent the system revolves around itself. Searches with the aim of establishing infringement of an existing patent or which check whether an invention is patentable belong within the system of obtaining and maintaining patents. They are not a use of the patent system but are rather part of the patent system itself. Much of the work of full-time patent searchers involves infringement and patentability searching (88).

Patentability searching involves a fairly thorough search in a small subject area going back as far as possible. The searcher is looking for evidence of lack of novelty or of non-obviousness of a given invention. The search will cover the subject matter of the invention and analogous subjects.

Infringement searching requires a narrow search only of patents within certain countries of interest and only during the period such patents could be in force. One is asking whether any patents would be infringed by carrying out certain activities and whether any known patents can be circumvented without infringing others. Therefore the search has to be entirely accurate or as close to this as possible,ie 100% recall. The precision, a measure of the percentage of relevant material, is not important and will inevitably be low to try and ensure a comprehensive coverage. For such a search it is important to use more than one classification scheme, search on keywords and use as many different indexes as is practicable. Each will be somewhat different and will increase coverage. The penalties involved in missing a relevant patent are wasted time and money in preparing for exploitation, forfeiture of goods, proceedings or threats of proceedings and possible damages for wrongful use. The firm may then end up having to pay a licence fee for use of the patent or may be banned from using it.

Licensing

Many patents are not exploited by their owners but are licensed to others. The patentee receives an income which must be negotiated along with conditions of use such as territorial or time restrictions or a requirement to liaise with other traders. Important components of such an agreement are the availability of additional know how and use of the information when the agreement comes to a end.

A licence may be exclusive, in which case the

licensee is allowed to exploit the invention to the exclusion of even the owner. If it is non-exclusive there will be competition either from the patentee alone or from a number of other licensees. Clearly the less competition, the more valuable is the licence. An intermediate position is the sole licensee, where the licensee competes only with the owner.

The EEC approves of intellectual property but has ruled that the IP rights with regard to any particular goods are exhausted once the patentee or licensee has put these particular goods on to the market. Therefore a licence may set up territorial restrictions: a French agent and a German agent may be appointed, but goods once sold must be allowed to move freely around the market. This means that goods sold by the French agent must be allowed to enter Germany and vice versa. These so-called parallel imports provide a minimum level of competition and no licence which would forbid parallel imports is likely to be allowed within the EEC. The present position is that the EEC has circulated a directive on patent licensing which outlines what would be permissible. There may yet be modifications but it gives the trend of their thinking. This is discussed further in Section 6.

Exchanging licences is part of industrial bargaining in many industries. Sometimes a patent pool is formed when a large amount of research is to be shared out among contributors. When such a pool breaks up there can be a great deal of litigation, for instance the series of cases between Beechams and Bristol Myers disputed world wide in the 1970s.

Employees' rights

A special category of inventor is the employee. An invention will belong to the employer if made in the course of normal work in a job which inventions are expected to be made. An invention also belongs to the employer in any situation where the employee is bound to safeguard the interests of the enterprise. This applies to senior management in positions of responsibility. In all other situations the invention belongs to the employee.

Thus far the 1977 Act agrees with and merely codifies previous law. An interesting new situation arises in that in any case where the employer holds a patent which is of exceptional value to the Company, the employee is entitled to statutory compensation. This is a highly ambiguous piece of legislation and so far there has been no case law (89). However, it has lead to some rewriting of contracts of employment so as to define exactly what work is being undertaken and whether the job requires inventiveness (90). A further implication is that clear project documentation should be maintained so that actual inventors can be identified. It will probably require one or two court cases to bring this home to the majority of industrial companies.

9.4 Exploitation of the Patent

At the stage of exploitation different categories of information will be required such as market research and introductions to manufacturers, prototype builders or financial institutions.

Large companies will have their own contacts, but much inventiveness springs from individuals working alone. Numerous organisations such as enterprise agencies and innovation centres exist to help. However they all need to assess the likelihood of commercial success as funds and other resources are limited and much depends on the initial presentation made by the inventor. Many ideas are rejected and they are unlikely to be all non-starters. Thus there is a gap at a crucial point in development. In the USA venture capital fills the gap but is not available so freely in Britain partly because of tax laws but also for many complex reasons of culture and expectations.

It has been suggested that a highly visible central agency is required to represent inventors and help them deal with other agents and with companies. This could well be the National Economic Development Organisation, NEDO. However these suggestions are as yet very preliminary.

Chapter 10   The Value of the Patent System

10.1 Theories of Patents

It has not and cannot be proved conclusively that
patent systems have any intrinsic value. However
there are a number of theories of patent systems
which seek to explain and justify them. In various
countries attitudes will depend much on political
instinct or dogma rather than on hard facts. There
are nevertheless a range of basic theories; the
favoured theory matching the political viewpoint
(91).

A. Reward to the inventor

The monopoly is given by the state as an
encouragement to inventors to reveal their ideas
rather than to keep them secret. Since the vast
majority of inventors are employees and the
decision to patent is taken by their employers,
this incentive is no longer of particular
importance.

B. Natural justice

Creative ideas naturally belong to their
originators. The award of a patent monopoly is the
fair reward given by the state in exchange for the
individual's creative effort. This attidude
influenced the systems in France and the USA
created after revolutions based on the primacy of
the individual. The theory is not very informative
as to further uses of the patents.

C. Economic theory

The economy must be stimulated by an influx of new
ideas. The only way to obtain them is to reward
their originators by way of patent monopolies.

This theory is subject to being turned on its head: patents restrict growth of the economy by exhibiting all the evils of monopolies.

D. A functioning information system

The patent system, by enforcing full disclosure of inventions, acts as a stimulus to the distribution of information to aid creativity. This is the only truly useful model. Over the last twenty years or so countries have improved the information content of patents by adopting deferred examination systems, involving publication of the application and by expanding the data available on front pages so that for increasing numbers of the community, both technical and commercial, patents are a valuable information source.

Internationally, the introduction of the PCT with its concept of minimum documentation was an important step forward. Also both the PCT and the EPC restrict the number of languages in which specifications will be published thus making it easier to read all the patents one needs to without requiring outside help.

10.2 Assessment of the System

It is impossible to establish the value of the patent system of any one country by experiment. If all countries abolished their patent laws and started afresh with a different system for handling inventions, one of these might be found to be just as good or even better than the present method. But the only evidence we do have is that of single countries surrounded by others with patent systems. Both Switzerland and the Netherlands had no patent systems during periods of active industrialisation. Both resumed granting patents under pressure from other countries. These are not fair tests as firms had access to the patent systems and published patents of other countries while granting no reciprocal privileges. It is likely that China enacted her recent patent law because of her desire for technology transfer from the West which was refused without patent protection.

Revision of the Paris Convention

Patents are undoubtedly valuable when they induce

technology transfer. However many lesser developed countries (LDCs) feel that they are exploited, as instead of transferring the technology, patents are used only to import the final product meanwhile stifling alternative attempts at development. There are provisions in the Convention for compulsory licences where a patent is not worked nationally for three years. But it is always open to the patentee then to start national working in order to swamp the market and put a compulsory licensee out of business again.

Therefore there is pressure from LDCs to change the Paris Convention. Two major proposals are

(i)   to lengthen the priority period from one to two years to allow more time to assemble information and test the market. This would benefit small enterprises in developed countries too.

(ii) when a compulsory licence is granted for non working, at the same time to take away the patentees' right to start to exploit the patent in that country.

There has been much discussion over a number of years on these proposals. Developed countries have threatened to split off if they are passed and LDCs to split off if they are not passed. Negotiations are slow and fitful but should result in a more equitable system in the end (92).

10.3   Alternatives to Patents

There has been much discussion in Britain and other countries about the connection between patenting and industrial output.

In Britain this has led to two developments.

A.The Green and White Papers

In December 1983 a Green Paper was published, it was called "Intellectual Property Rights and Innovation" (93). It looks at awareness, accessibility and use of intellectual property, coverage and consistency of rights and use and abuse of rights.

It looks at intellectual property as a whole

rather than in watertight compartments and makes many administrative suggestions such as to turn the Patent Office into an independent statutory body like the Civil Aviation Authority. This may or may not have a noticeable effect. It also recommends various small changes in law to extend protection and make the system more attractive to potential users. The so called privatisation of the patent office has been adopted as policy by the Government in 1986. There has been a White Paper based on this Green Paper and on copyright issues and legislation may result (94).

In the field of patents, major recommendations have concerned simplifying the procedures of litigation and ending the patent agents' monopoly. More litigation may be started and finished in the Patent Office and not reach the High Court (where the costs mount up) without special permission. The monopoly enjoyed by patent agents on writing specifications and representing clients (shared with solicitors) is being examined by the Office of Fair Trading. It is argued by some that other skilled professionals such as accountants could do this work or parts of it without needing much special training. An intermediate step short of relaxing the monopoly would be to allow agents to practise with a shorter training period and a simpler qualification.

The main recommendations for our purposes are those dealing with information and awareness. The Patent Office should attempt to make industry (and Whitehall) more aware of the valuable information contained in patents for technical, commercial and market intelligence. However it makes no mention of online retrieval systems nor of the increasing amount of study of law and policy in this area now taking place. One result of these comments is that the Patent Office has set up an awareness unit which will try to reach out to industry and educate potential users (95).

B. Innovation protection

It has been argued that the patent system protects the wrong part of the innovation process. It is too early and protects something which could be the root of a variety of products. Innovation protection is intended to protect a specific product while it is being developed for the

market. An innovation will qualify for protection
if a particular product is not available
nationally (eg electric cars). Then the entire
programme up to marketing will be protected.
Kingston writes that the lifetime of the monopoly
should be measured in terms of profit recovered.
After a fixed multiple of the outlay is earned in
sales the monopoly would lapse (96). The EEC
Commission has examined the organisational and
informational consequences of such a regime (97).
It is likely that the information quid pro quo to
a development monopoly could be very rich as it
would reveal blueprints and detailed instructions
currently termed "unknown". But no industry would
be likely to agree to publish these freely so that
complex provisions would need to be made for what
is to be published and what can be held back
perhaps with some supervised rights of access.

SECTION 3   INDUSTRIAL COPYRIGHT AND DESIGNS

Chapter 1   Basic Principles of Copyright in the UK

Copyright law provides the means for regulating the use of creative works. The law in Britain is currently given by the Copyright Act of 1956 with amendments (1).

1.1   Brief History

The need for protection from copying arose with the invention of printing (2). From 1586 up to 1694 members of the Stationers' Company were the only people who could print or import books. Authors had to assign their common law right of control of their works to a member of the Company who would register himself (or his company) as having the printing monopoly for those works. Each assignment carried with it a perpetual copyright but this was not a "modern" type of protection.

In return for the monopoly, the Stationers' Company enforced first the religious and then the political censorship desired by the Government. By 1694 there was no perceived need for censorship any more, but the evils of monopoly power were glaringly obvious and so Parliament abolished the monopoly.

For a few years chaos reigned and then in 1709 the Statute of Anne, the first modern Copyright Act was passed. It gave the author the right to control who would print the work for up to 28 years. The Stationers' Company would still register books before publication but the printer no longer had to be one of their members. Pirate copies were forfeit to the copyright owner with fines to the owner and to the state. Unpublished works were not included in this Act.

From then on, copyright law proceeded by a continuous accretion of statutes. The following changes were made:

(a) The duration of copyright was extended to include all of the author's life and then to benefit the heirs as well.

(b) Separate laws were enacted to bring in other types of work such as fine arts, sculpture and music. These laws were finally included in one unified Act in 1911.

(c) Unpublished works were included in the statutory protection.

(d) Reproductive technologies other than printing were brought into the scope of the law. These included broadcasting, audio and video recording, photographs and films, photocopying, cable services and material in electronic codes.

and (e) Registration was abolished.

Finally the Act of 1956 was passed and is current with one or two provisions dating from 1911 still in force. There are also a number of later amending Acts dealing with specific topics.

1.2   The Copyright Act 1956

The 1956 Act protects two separate entities.

Part 1 deals with "works" which are literary, dramatic, musical or artistic creations. They must be "original", which means that the precise form in which an idea is expressed must have been created by the author. Note that original does not mean novel as it does with patents. The contents will usually be well worn material, it is the tangible form which is protected. In theory the idea is left free although the distinction is somewhat imprecise. Copyright vests in the author of a work from the moment of its creation.

Part 2 deals with manifestations of works such as printed editions, films and audio and video recordings. Control is given to their maker or publisher.

Restricted acts

Certain actions may be carried out only by the copyright owner or with his permission.

The main ones are:

> Reproducing the work in any material form,
>
> Publishing the work, which means selling copies to the public,
>
> Making any adaptation to the work such as a translation or a re-working of a novel into a television play,
>
> Performing the work in public,
>
> Broadcasting the work, and
>
> Including it in a cable programme.

These apply to original works in Part 1 but not to derivative works in Part 2, each of which has its own list of restricted activities appropriate to its nature (similar to those above). One work may have several copyrights associated with it covering different aspects and each with a different owner. Copyright in this sense means the right attached to one aspect of one work as granted under a Copyright Act.

In general, the duration of Part 1 copyright for published works is life of the author plus fifty years. For Part 2, the term is fifty years from the date of first production except for printed editions where it is twenty-five years from first printing. Note that these terms leave unpublished works with perpetual copyright. The clock begins to tick only when the first publication takes place.

Prospects for reform

The Copyright Act 1956 has become rather out of date in various ways. In 1974 a Committee was set up under Mr Justice Whitford to report on possible reforms. Its report in 1977 was a detailed and authoritative one but was left such a time that it has been long out of date (3). In 1981 a Green Paper was published partly agreeing, partly disagreeing, with the Whitford report (4).

Pressure for particular reforms has been mounting. Reports have been written on taping (5) and on industrial designs (6), and piecemeal reforms were implemented concerning damages for piracy (7) and protection for computer programs (8).

A White Paper was published in 1986 (9). It does not outline a completely new law of copyright but it deals with all the points of controversy in a systematic manner. Its main aim is to make the law as consistent as possible across all the different interests.

Industrial copyright

The handling of one-off creative products is outside the context of this book. Copyright also encompasses the protection of mass produced objects of utility when they have an original and aesthetically appealing or distinctive appearance. The borderline between art and utility is an unclear one at best.

There are two aspects to utilitarian art. One originates from artistic craftsmanship. Talented great names like Wedgwood drew pictures for chinaware, William Morris designed wallpaper and tiles and Hepplewhite carved chairs. Objects like chairs are designated works of artistic craftsmanship in their entirety. This category would also cover a designer dress for instance. In the case of a drawing applied to a plate, tile, wallpaper or any other saleable object, the original drawing is protected by copyright as an artistic work. Industrial use is defined as application to more than fifty items or printing of more than a certain length of wallpaper or fabrics. There is a separate design copyright which applies to the artistic work as applied to an object for industrial use. The applied work is called a "corresponding design".

Copyright protection for an artistic work or for a work of artistic craftsmanship lasts for the normal length of the artist's life plus fifty years. When either of these types of work is mass produced, the design copyright lasts for fifteen years only. This will be described further in conjunction with registered designs.

The second aspect is that engineering plans and technical drawings are protected as artistic works. This is because a "drawing" is defined as including images and plans. If they are original drawings no other attribute is required such as "artistry". An enactment unique to British copyright law is that the three dimensional embodiment of a two dimensional drawing is an infringement of the copyright in the drawing. Therefore any object made from drawings is protected by copyright providing only that a "lay" eye could see that the object was made according to the instructions of the drawing. Protection would logically be for the lifetime of the draughtsman plus fifty years.

To sum up; industrial objects are protected if made from existing technical drawings, or if they are objects of craftsmanship in their own right, or if they embody a corresponding design (a pattern printed on a mug or on a T-shirt for instance).

This adds up to quite a formidable protection. It is not quite as strong as it looks because of modification by the Registered Designs Act. Before coming to that, let us look at some examples of industrial copyright.

L B Plastics v Swish Products Ltd (10)

This design concerned the copying of self-assembly drawers to be used in furniture carcasses manufactured by a third party. Since the nature and shape of the drawers was determined by their function and the carcass itself, the scope for variation was very limited. Swish Products had seen drawings of the drawers made by LB Plastics, and evidence showed that they had checked for the existence of patents or registered designs and then adopted the broad concept of the design before them even though there had been scope for a different approach. Since Swish had seen and acted upon the plaintiffs' drawings, the House of Lords decided that Swish had copied the product as depicted in those drawings. This was an important judgment, as there was much discussion of what is form and what is merely the idea of compatible drawers, which should remain freely available.

Hensher v Restawhile (11)

This case concerned a new style of chairs manufactured from a prototype with no drawings. The plaintiff could claim copyright protection only as a form of artistic craftsmanship. The defendants conceded that the furniture was made through the exercise of craftsmanship, but argued that the chairs were not artistic.

Like LB Plastics v Swish this case went to the House of Lords. The question at stake was how to define artistic craftsmanship in an object; the general view was a subjective one: the appearance of the chairs must be aesthetically attractive and give people pleasure. Only one judge wished to ask an objective question ; "is the constructor an artist-craftsman as understood?" It was held in this case that the chairs were not in fact works of artistic craftsmanship, but this could have stemmed from a class and generation gap as the chairs were flashy and attractive to young and probably working class people, rather than to the judiciary. This exposes the rather uncertain basis of the artistic craftsmanship designation where there is no consensus as to artistic quality.

Solar Thompson v Barton (12)

This case concerns the attempted use of the "layman's defence" : that a layman would not have been able to relate the defendant's product to the plaintiff's drawings. Here the product was a pulley wheel. Since the drawings were cross-sections, a relationship between them and the product was difficult to establish. The judge ruled that one should assume the layman held a cross-section of the pulley in his hand. This rather emasculates the layman's defence as one needs considerable expertise to interpret drawings. As this decision was given by the Court of Appeal it carries considerable weight.

These three cases give some idea of the application of copyright law to an industrial context.

Penalties and their enforcement

If copyright infringement is proved, the infringer normally has to deliver up all infringing items and/or pay a sum of money. This money may take the form of compensatory damages related to loss, or it could be determined by an account of profits. In addition, there is another form of damages, called conversion damages, unique to copyright. These are calculated as the entire value of an object based on the concept that the object belongs to the copyright owner and was effectively stolen (converted) by the infringer. Thus if an infringing design is printed onto T-shirts one pays the value of the shirt, if it is stamped onto a gold nugget one has to pay for the gold nugget as imprinted. However, a T-shirt becomes much more valuable with a pattern, while a gold nugget is already valuable and a pattern adds only a little. This factor is ignored at present, and therefore the price paid does not really reflect the value of the right which has been infringed. It makes copyright an attractive form of property to its owners. But the damages are generally regarded as excessive and are out of line with awards from other types of civil action. Therefore, the 1986 White Paper recommends abolition of conversion damages.

1.3 Registered Designs Legislation

The extent of copyright protection for industrial designs outlined above is quite impressive. Protection is long lasting and automatic, but it is not ideal.

In general, drawings are required in order to protect a three dimensional object. Protection is given only for precisely the same design, therefore it is often easy to avoid liability while taking the main idea. Also only copying is prevented, convergent but separately conceived designs are allowed.

For consumers the long duration of copyright is also not particularly desirable. It means virtually lifelong protection for industrial products, which can stifle creativity. One may, of course, design around a protected work, but there is a big difference between copying as closely as one dares and creative extension of a work. Such extension requires commitment and effort and any hint of a legal barrier at the end is likely to prevent a project from even starting. This is the hidden aspect by which copyright damages creativity.

What seems to be required to meet the interests
both of industrial competitors and the consumer is
a short term protection for a design that is novel
rather than original. That means not produced by
anyone else at all. The protection should be aimed
at any use of the design, not just copying.

These requirements are satisfied by the **Registered
Designs Act 1949** (13). Prior to 1949 designs
legislation was part of patent law and only then
separated. It is a hybrid between patent and
copyright concepts.

Design is defined as being features of shape and
distinctive appearance which are to be judged by
eye and applied industrially. Methods or
principles of construction are excluded as are any
configurations dictated solely by function.
Essentially literary or artistic works are also
excluded.

A novelty search against previous British designs
is carried out by the Designs Registry on
application. Protection is then given for fifteen
years in three periods of five years (14). The
White Paper suggests increasing this to twenty-
five years but making the eye appeal condition
more stringent.

The **Designs Registry** is a closed access office.
The public can request a search (with fee) by
giving the name of a company or individual, a
registration number if it is known or a subject.

It was long assumed that practically all
industrial objects with a distinctive appearance
could have their design registered. The limitation
against function would hardly ever apply as there
can always be very slight variations even in
highly constrained objects such as aeroplane
wings. However, the understanding was restricted
by case law to mean objects which are bought with
their appearance in mind only. If the appearance
is irrelevant then the object is to be treated as
purely functional.

Relationship between the Design and Copyright Acts

Between 1949 and 1957, the Copyright Act of 1911 stated that designs used industrially had protection only under the Registered Designs Act and were excluded from the scope of the Copyright Act. If used but not registered they had no protection.

Between 1957 and 1968 all artistic works such as drawings and sculptures were protected under the 1956 Copyright Act and the owner could sue anyone who infringed the copyright whether in two dimensions or three. But if a corresponding design was registered under the Registered Designs Act, then acts falling within the scope of design copyright were removed from the scope of the Copyright Act. They were protected for up to 15 years as designs and then unprotected. Meanwhile the protection of the Copyright Act continued for all non-industrial uses. If a design was marketed but not registered then industrial use protection was lost entirely.

In 1968 the Design Copyright Act was enacted (15). From then on the protection under CA 1956 continues parallel to design protection so that a work is covered whether or not it is registered. This was done for the benefit of small industrial users such as costume jewellers who maintained that the cost and time involved in registration were not worth their while with very short runs.

The picture now seems to be clear, we have artistic objects protected under copyright including three dimensional copying, and we have dual copyright and design protection for industrial production. There is one more category: industrial production where a design cannot be registered.

1.4 Non-registrable Designs

The tangle of laws and cases in this area have produced an awkward anomaly (16).

The Registered Designs Act provides that designs dictated by their function cannot be registered. So what, if any, protection do such designs attract?

This was answered in 1965 by the case of **Dorling v Honnor Marine** (17). The case concerned plans for a kit of parts for a sailing dinghy. These parts were treated as being essentially functional and the plans incapable of registration. But the House of Lords decided that some protection must still be afforded. Therefore the drawings being original works of the draughtsman were held to attract artistic copyright and be protected for the lifetime of the draughtsman plus fifty years.

This is the first and primary anomaly, the provision of such a disproportionately long protection for functional objects. However it was not thought to be too important as this was a small class of objects.

The class of these objects was greatly widened by the House of Lords in an important decision of 1972: **Amp v Utilux** (18). This concerned rights in an electric plug. The House of Lords judgment held that the design was not registrable, not because its shape was fixed by function but because the shape was irrelevant. No one buys an electrical fitting for its appearance they reasoned, only for its function. Therefore the shape even if it varied was still purely functional and registration was denied.

This decision dramatically increased the number of excluded items from an unimportant small group to the majority of all mass produced goods. They were deemed by the legislation to be less worthy of merit by virtue of being functional and having no eye appeal. This in itself was a very dubious and arguable assumption. The result was that these "inferior" objects attract long and secure copyright protection while artistic objects are given fifteen years only whether or not they register. A minefield indeed. Both the Whitford Report and the Green Paper recommended abolishing the functional/non-functional divide and giving a uniform short protection to all mass produced objects. This idea stems from the Johnson Report of 1962 which was concerned with industrial designs. However, as yet nothing has been done.

Whitford J tried to take the initiative by applying yet more case law. In the case of **Hoover**

v Hulme (19) in 1982 he argued that Amp v Utilux had misinterpreted the law, that the fifteen years protection under the Design Copyright Act of 1968 depended only on whether a design was used industrially, not whether it was registrable. Under this interpretation, all industrially used designs would have only fifteen years protection either as a registered design or under copyright.

This judgment would have solved the problem. However it was at the High Court level only and although that case was not appealed it was later reconsidered and overruled by the Court of Appeal and House of Lords in **BL Cars v Armstrong Patents Co** (20).

This case dealt with the spare parts industry, the main beneficiary of this industrial copyright anomaly. There are many firms which specialise in making spare parts for common equipment and these now have to pay royalties to the originators of the equipment for use of their copyrights. These are quite high: British Leyland charges 7% of the selling price. The legality of this whole procedure (plus the royalty rate) was established by this case. Armstrong made exhausts to fit BL's cars but refused to pay the royalty. The High Court and Court of Appeal affirmed that the exhaust pipes were copies of the drawings and that BL held the copyright. The House of Lords has now overturned this but in narrow circumstances only. Their reasons were not related to copyright but to an owner's right to have his car repaired wherever he wished and at a reasonable price. They did regret the strangle-hold of copyright on industrial design work but held that legislation is required to change the balance.

In a separate "Euro defence" Armstrong also claimed that BL was abusing its dominant position in the market. However it was established that there were many licensees all willing to pay the 7% royalty and that their combined competition had forced BL to lower its own prices. In light of this, the Court held that there was no attempt to dominate the market and this claim was also dismissed.

Reforms

Removing protection from three dimensional objects constructed from two dimensional plans would reduce the industrial copyright anomaly. Apart from that, the whole question of the split between "pure" art and utilitarian design has to be examined. The White Paper proposes an unregistered design right lasting ten years for all non-registrable goods (21).

Other countries treat these two aspects in a variety of different ways. Because of the pressure for EEC harmonisation, it is necessary to study these approaches and try to abstract best practice.

Chapter 2 Industrial Copyright in Other Countries

2.1 The EEC

Apart from the Irish Republic, no EEC countries other than the UK allow three dimensional protection from a two dimensional base. Objects are protected on their own merits. There are three basic approaches to the split between copyrights and designs (22).

1) UK and France profess the doctrine of unity of art, that all original drawings are on a continuum of more or less artistic value. Therefore protection is available to all of them.

2) In Italy protection of industrial products via design is entirely dissociated from protection of art. The artistic element in a product will get copyright protection if it can be dissociated from the product.

3) West Germany and the Benelux countries distinguish art from design. There must be artistic merit for an object to attract copyright protection, but if it has that merit the object can also be functional.

The differences between the laws of each country are complex, each falls into one of the three broad categories as exemplified above.

Issues to be considered are:

1) Need for two types of protection.

2) Need for either complete dissociation or complete cumulation. Distinctions based on level of art are too subjective and artificial to be relied upon.

3)   Need to eliminate "moral rights" from
     industrial copyright. These inalienable
     rights barely exist in Britain but are strong
     in most of Europe. An author is allowed to
     object to changes or to withdraw a work from
     circulation if he feels that it now reflects
     badly on his style and reputation.This is
     inappropriate in an industrial context.

Most EEC countries also have unfair competition
laws which impinge upon the copyright issue in its
wider policy aspects.

It would appear that differences are too great for
voluntary harmonisation. Various countries are
thinking of national reform but an EEC-wide
supranational law seems unlikely in the near
future as much time and effort would need to be
devoted to its preparation.

2.2 The USA

Designs in the US are treated as a branch of
patent law (23).   Standards of originality and
novelty are very high. A design patent gives
fourteen years of protection but is difficult to
enforce because of the high standards imposed by
the Courts. Unfair competition and trade secret
laws are more useful.

Ornamentation separate from function could be
given copyright protection, but not the shape of
an object as such. Technical drawings are
protected as drawings but these on their own
protect little of importance. The US system is
sufficiently different to that in Europe to be of
little assistance in resolving European
differences.

Chapter 3   International Protection

As with all forms of industrial property, the international dimension is of vital importance.

3.1 Copyright

This is controlled by two international conventions (24):

The Berne Convention of 1886 administered by WIPO in Geneva; and The Universal Copyright Convention (UCC) of 1952 administered by UNESCO in Paris.

The UK is a member of both. The UCC was a breakaway from Berne providing less protection for authors and encouraging greater mobility of works. It was set up by less developed countries more concerned with importing external knowledge and culture than with disseminating their own.

The **Berne Convention** has three basic principles.

1)   Works of nationals of member states and works first published in such states must be given the same protection in any state as that state gives to the work of its own nationals.

2)   Full protection must be given. No refusal is allowed on the grounds of lack of reciprocity.

3)   Protection is automatic upon creation of a work. There are no formalities.

There are also three minimum requirements:

International Protection

1) "Every production in the literary, scientific and artisitic domain whatever the mode or form of its expression" is to be protected.

2) Rights for the copyright owner must include reproduction rights, translation, adaptation and arrangement rights, performing rights and broadcasting and film rights.

3) Duration of copyright must be at least the life of the author plus fifty years.

This package adds up to very powerful protection for authors. Note that only UK Part 1 works are considered here. Part 2 rights are called "neighbouring rights" and are enshrined in other conventions. They are secondary to the creative act and there is no logical reason to include them under copyright.

The **UCC** retains the principle of national protection: the same protection for foreign works as for national ones, but it does allow for reciprocity. If a particular right does not exist in one country, another member of the UCC need not grant that right to works originating from that country. Combining this with national protection, a country can grant to foreign works either the same rights as it grants its nationals, or no rights at all. It cannot grant a set of rights with provisions which differ depending on the country of origin of a work.

The biggest difference between the two conventions is that UCC countries like the USA can require formalities to be completed as a condition of protection. They can set up a register and only grant protection to duly registered works. A great contribution of UCC is that for foreigners, it is agreed that the formalities are satisfied if the author includes in each item the copyright symbol "C" in a circle, the date of first publication and the name of the copyright owner.The state can specify additional procedures but only nationals and permanent residents need to comply with them.

If the UCC symbols are seen in British books, it is not because they are required for UK copyright, but in case an edition is sold in the USA or any other UCC country.

The minimum requirements for UCC are very minimal. They merely require adequate protection to be given with a lifetime of not less than twenty-five years.
Many countries are members of both conventions and virtually all countries are a member of one or the other. There are 76 states in Berne and 77 in the UCC. Members of both conventions apply the weaker UCC rules solely with respect to UCC-only countries.

A number of amendments have been made to each convention. The latest being joint enactment of rights in favour of developing countries agreed in Paris in 1971.

For our purposes it is sufficient to be aware of the broad provisions and the principles behind them. Requirements for any one state are best looked up when needed.

3.2 Designs

These are protected under the Paris Convention of 1883 which deals with all industrial property. There is a six months convention period for application for an industrial design in any other member state of the Convention (25).

Unlike patent laws, designs legislation is likely to require local relative novelty rather than worldwide absolute novelty. Therefore the international convention is of less importance. However some products are internationally known and do require wide protection. For instance the "Anglepoise" lamp can be bought from the UK to Australia and back again.

Export furnishings and fabrics, "get up" of products such as drugs, electrical goods, machinery etc are all known and sold worldwide.

We have discussed how design seems to fall between patent and copyright concepts. It also meshes with trade marks which are concerned with the distinctive marking and appearance of one supplier's goods.

Trade marks are the next logical topic for us to consider.

SECTION 4 TRADE MARKS

Chapter 1   Introduction to Trade Marks

A trade mark is a mark placed on goods to indicate who made or sold them. Strictly they are a means of relating a product to its supplier so that a purchaser can choose to buy the goods from one source rather than another. The mark is not intended to give an assurance of quality but it often does so indirectly as a purchaser buys the goods of one source rather than another in reliance on its reputation. This intangible business reputation is known as goodwill (1).

There are two types of mark: informal and formal. The informal type should strictly be termed a trade name and the formal type a registered trade mark or RTM. Both types will be described. The discussion will centre mainly on marks placed on goods. In most other countries RTMs have also been available for services, such as dry cleaners or banks but in Britain services have had only the lesser informal protection. Recently the Trade Marks Act 1938 (2) has been amended to allow service marks (3), the registration of which commenced in late 1986. In most respects their treatment will be the same as for marks on goods.

Registered trade marks are of great value to their owners. Once granted they can potentially be used for ever. Their business significance arises with respect to advertising (4). Because an RTM cements the relationship between goods and their supplier, the advertising can concentrate on creating an image which may be irrelevant to the product as such. An example of this is men playing games or performing feats of strength and then drinking beer. A psychological connection is being attempted between beer and a way of life. In this way the establishment of RTMs has had a vast but largely unrecognised effect on everyday lives. Without a trade mark, such advertisements would need to concentrate on linking enjoyment of the beer with that particular supplier and there would be less opportunity to create images. Informal marks also free the advertiser from the need to emphasise his name, but are less effective since the connection is less well defined. This difference will become clearer when we consider the nature of the protection conferred.

Trade marks are of less interest to information scientists than are patents because they convey no technical information (except for certification trade marks which are an untypical subgroup dealt with towards the end of 2.1). They can be used to relate a product known only by its trade mark to its producer via the register. However the main uses of trade mark information are circular ones such as looking through existing trade marks when thinking of a new name for a new product. Also one should keep an eye on new registrations in order to detect any that come "close" to one's own either orally or visually. As RTMs are classified by the goods they are applied to, only related areas need be searched. The classification marks for goods are very broad, but applicants are expected to give much more detail so that the use of a mark is quite closely delimited.

By definition, only a registered trade mark can be searched on the official register. In many countries only RTMs are given any protection at all. In Britain and the US, informal trade names are also protected but the level of protection is much less definite than for RTMs and each case is treated on its merits.

Chapter 2   Trade Mark Law in Britain

2.1   Registered Trade Marks

These are at present governed by the Trade Marks
Act of 1938.

The first law establishing RTMs in the UK was
passed in 1876. Prior to 1876 one had to rely on
the common law of deception to deal with false
indications of origins of goods. The action
arising from the common law is called passing off
and is still used in the protection of
unregistered trade names.

Procedure

Under the 1938 Act , to have a mark registered one
submits an application form along with a sample of
the mark in symbols and words, and a statement of
the goods on which it has been or is intended to
be used. The Registry carries out a novelty search
through existing RTMs, looking for any similar
marks for similar goods; the presence of such
marks may prejudice or ultimately prevent
registration. Prior use of the mark is encouraged,
or at least not discouraged (5). There are also a
number of general criteria which the Registry must
consider. To be eligible for registration a mark:

> must be distinctive
> must not be deceptive
> must not be descriptive
> and must not fit in one of a number of
> specifically excluded categories.

1.   Distinctiveness

There are two levels of distinctiveness available

for UK trade marks; Part A and Part B. The requirement for Part B is lower than that set for Part A and the level of protection provided is consequently lower.

Distinctiveness means that the mark must be associated in the minds of those in the trade with the particular goods. The mark must be associated not with the goods as such but with the goods as produced by the owner of that mark. Furthermore, the association must be specifically between the owner and those goods, not a generalised connection which could be used by another trader and his goods (such as a place name). These considerations apply equally to services. The main concern is not to rob the English language of words of general applicability.

An invented word is frequently the most suitable type of mark for which to seek registration. As it has no connotations at all, it will inevitably be distinctive of the goods in question as soon as it is used. Therefore prior use is not required to establish distinctiveness. Examples of such marks are KODAK and SCHWEPPES.

Symbols are useful as trade marks, but the word itself is the more important since this would be spoken or written when orders are placed.

Once a word has connotations, then distinctiveness has to be established by use. Examples here are:

> common names: SMITH'S CRISPS
> numbers: HEINZ'S 57 VARIETIES
> single letters: K SHOES

In these cases the letters or numbers are only protected as drawn. There must be a disclaimer as to rights over the letter, number or name in general.

Part A marks have to be highly distinctive of their product. They consist mainly of invented words or of words that have been long in use. They are infringed by any unauthorised use in trade. Such a blanket restriction would clearly be unjustified if there were legitimate uses to which a word could be put.

For Part B a lower level of distinctiveness is permitted. This is suitable for words with connotations. They may be upgraded to Part A later. Actual or likely misleading of the public is required for a Part B mark. There is no difference in fees or length of protection between Parts A and B.

2. Deceptiveness

A mark must not be deceptive. That means that it must not be too similar in spelling, sound or appearance to another mark in the same field.

Two judgments have to be made with regard to deceptiveness of a mark intended for registration. First of all, is the word really close to another word? This must include the sound as spoken. For instance, GALAXY was regarded as being too close to GLAXO. The second decision is: are the names being used in the same field? In the above example "galaxy" was used for chocolate while "glaxo" labelled a wider range of milk products. These were regarded as being the same field of endeavour. As a counter example inboard engines for pleasure boats and outboard motors for ocean ships have been held to be in different fields.

An identical name can freely be used on different products. SUSAN has been used on kettles, matches and fountain pens for instance. This is permissible because the public has no cause to imagine a commercial relationship between the manufacturers of such diverse objects. Therefore there is no room for confusion.

3. Descriptiveness

A mark must not describe the product or indicate its attributes. If such a description were appropriated by one user it would proscribe routine marketing activities by others, by associating general descriptive characteristics with one manifestation. For instance the PRESTEL service which uses telephones coupled to TV sets to display a library of information put up by many independent suppliers, initially tried to register the name VIEWDATA. This was clearly too descriptive. Others that failed to register are:

MINIGROOVE for records
EARTHMASTER for a mechanical shovel, and
AUTOANALYZER for analysis apparatus.

The decision as to whether these names are truly descriptive is a difficult one to take. They are not words one would use as such in normal conversation. Some contentious ones get through like BABY BUGGY for a child's collapsible pushchair and ANSAFONE for a telephone answering machine.

4. Excluded categories

There are a number of types of words not allowed to be registered as trade marks, although they may be used.

a)   No common surnames are allowed. The London telephone directory gives an indication of frequencies. Existing use of the name is taken into account as this might have created a level of distinctiveness in practice.

The name of a company or an individual represented in a special manner such as by a signature is allowed. In such a case the actual name would be disclaimed, only the particular format in use being protected. An identifiable and living individual must give permission before their name or portrait can be used. Otherwise they could sue for libel.

b)   No geographical place names are allowed. This rule is applied far more rigidly than that covering personal names. An obscure foreign place name might be permitted if sufficiently obscure that most people would not recognise it as a place. A series of judgments has established that a well known place name cannot be registered even if it has been established as 100% distinctive in fact. The most recent of these is the **York Trailers** case. The firm concerned manufactured vehicles in York, was the only one to do so and to use the town name of York as the main part of their name and had therefore achieved 100% distinctiveness. But a trade mark registration lasts potentially for ever and would exclude other vehicle makers from attaching the town name to their products. It was the need to protect future rights that led to the refusal of this application.

c)   No names of colours are permitted as such. They may be incorporated as part of a wider mark, for instance BLACK MAGIC.

Other proscribed categories are
d)   No royal connotations such as crowns and flags.

e)   No obscene or offensive words.

f)   No words contrary to law or morality.

g)   No words which could give rise to false expectations. An example of falsehood was given by the word ORLWOOLA which was held to be either descriptive for a woollen garment or false for one containing artificial fibres.

Once a mark has been accepted it is advertised in the Official Journal of Trade Marks; OJ(TM). There is a one month period during which opposition to the grant may be notified. Once this period is over or when any opposition has been dealt with, the mark is formally entered on the Register. It is initially in force for seven years. Renewal is then for fourteen years at a time as long as the mark is used.

Use of an RTM

The proprietor will normally use a mark himself and it is possible to allow one or more registered users (licensees) to use the mark as well. Licensing is more complex than with patents because of the need to associate the mark with the goods and the goodwill of their source.

Attempts have been made to widen use for certain types of trading. A particular and major example of this is **character merchandising** (6). Here a character is taken from fiction or from films and television and sold as a doll or drawn on writing paper, cups, tee shirts and similar items. Sometimes pop stars and sportsmen are given similar treatment. Attempts to have such symbols registered as trade marks have foundered on the diversity of goods. This is called traffiking, trading in the mark rather than the merchandise. It is strongly disapproved of and in the decision concerning **Holly Hobbie**, the House of Lords ruled that such symbols were not registrable (7). Thus nearly all character merchandising is carried out informally and the topic will be dealt with in 2.2.

An RTM may be kept in force as long as it is used on a product or on the producer's letter heads, bills and so on. If there has been no use for five years or more, any interested third party can apply to have the mark removed from the Register. The device or word is normally marked in some way to make it stand out as a registered trade mark. "Reg" or "TM" are common forms but there are no rules about this. If a third party refers to an RTM there is likewise no rule as to how this is to be done, only that some acknowledgment must be made.

Infringement

For a Part A RTM, any unauthorised use in the course of trade constitutes infringement whether it damages the trade mark propagator or not. For a Part B mark, actual or potential damage must be demonstrated and this is also true for actions for infringement of non-registered marks (8). "Use" can involve not only imitation of a mark but also comparative advertising or referral to another's product by its trade mark in promotional literature.

If infringement is proved, the usual range of remedies available includes an injunction against further infringement, confiscation of goods and damages based on loss of profits or effect on reputation as appropriate.

Cancellation of registration

A mark can be removed from the register for a number of reasons:

1. Registration is not renewed. This could be because it is no longer required, but could also be due to an oversight. The interval between renewals is fourteen years and it could be forgotten. A firm might have changed hands and the records been mislaid. The registry does issue renewal notices. These are sent to the last notified address of the proprietor or to an agent if one is appointed. The long interval leaves plenty of opportunity for error to creep in. The most common problem is that the proprietor moves and does not notify his change of address.

Often RTMs are obtained with the assistance of a trade mark agent. A firm of agents can retain responsibility for a mark and undertake to remind the proprietor of renewal dates. Nevertheless, if a firm has changed address it may no longer be traceable. In this way a mark can be lost and its proprietor may be quite unaware of the fact.

2. Lack of use. This has been discussed above. Non-use over five years is enough to disqualify a mark.

3. Wrongly registered. It is possible to allege at any time that a trade mark was wrongly registered. For marks in Part A of the Register, the registration cannot be challenged after the first seven years unless it was obtained by fraud or if the mark as used would be likely to deceive, cause confusion, be scandalous or contrary to law or morality, or be "disentitled to protection in a court of justice". These provisions are rather open ended and subjective and their use, sometimes after many years, to disqualify a mark is rather controversial.

Part B marks can be challenged at any time on any aspect of their registration. However it is envisaged that any mark would transfer to Part A as soon as it had acquired through use sufficient distinctiveness to be allowed to do so.

4. The mark becomes generic. A trade mark is intended to act as a brand name for a subset of goods of one type. It sometimes happens that the trade mark becomes the name used indiscriminately for all goods of that type and loses its ability to distinguish between sources. A famous example is BIRO. If a customer asks for a "biro", does the customer expect to receive, and the shop assistant to provide, a ball point pen made by a particular firm or just any ball point pen?

When a mark becomes generic it is clearly unusable as a trade mark and will be removed from the register upon application by a third party.

More examples of generics are ASPIRIN, CELLULOID, ESCALATOR, HOVERCRAFT, NYLON, UNDERSEAL and GRIPE WATER.

Some potential generics are HOOVER, THERMOS, SELLOTAPE, BABY BUGGY, DUREX, FORMICA, XEROX and TANNOY.

Trade mark proprietors are caught in a contradiction: they like their particular names to be publicised in all popular media which could bring the product to public attention. But they must immediately reprimand the publishers or others if they do not stress that the word is a trade mark owned by them and not a common name. Prompt action prevents or slows down careless use of such names and is the price to pay for exclusivity.

Special trade marks

There are a few special categories of mark which do not wholly follow the above rules but are still types of trade mark.

1. Defensive trade marks

These are RTMs which are so associated with high quality goods that they are protected in all classes of goods. Normally trade marks are only distinctive in use on the type of goods with which they are normally used. But statements like "a Rolls Royce kettle" or "a Rolls Royce system of management", carry connotations of quality whether or not the mark is used or usable in the given category. Hence the global protection. Such marks are very rare as it is difficult to prove the need. Examples include ST MICHAEL, ROLLS ROYCE, OXO, TYPHOO and HOVIS. Only invented words are eligible for defensive protection.

It is also possible to extend registration only partially to cover only a range of related classes. This is a rather more frequently used form of defensive registration.

2. Certification trade marks

These are issued by an independent non-trading owner to denote a standard of quality.

There must be a set of regulations laying down how the mark is to be used and the standard to be complied with. These have to be approved by the Department of Trade and Industry and are available for inspection at the Trade Mark Office in London.

The mark is then issued to authorised users who can build up a substantial marketing reputation. Examples are HARRIS TWEED cloth, STILTON cheese, ENGLISH WINE and the British Standards Institution's KITE-MARK.

Certification trade marks differ from other marks in that they can convey technical information. This would be presented in the regulations which lay down what is to be complied with in order to use the mark. For instance British Standards are often incorporated into kite-marked products. As a source of information they are practically unexploited, but the potential is considerable.

2.2   Unregistered Trade Marks

These are any names, marks or general get-up given to goods or services by traders and used just as RTMs are used in advertising and promotion of goods.   A mark may be used and then registered or it may never be registered, either through lack of eligibility or through lack of motivation.

If a reputation has been established, then the rights of use of a mark will be protected by common law to prevent deception. There are no written guidelines, only previous cases to guide the judges.

The main problems when protecting an unregistered mark are

    a) to prove a reputation in the mark
    b) to prove that damage or potential damage will
       occur.

The matter of reputation is identical to that of

an RTM before registration. Evidence of length of use and exposure of the mark can be backed up with survey evidence from members of the public or the trade to establish recognition of a mark or confusion with another.

The second problem is the more difficult one. If the disputed mark is used in a manner different from the original, then the question of common field of activity must be raised. Evidence of damage will be accepted only if the two activities are in the same field of commercial endeavour. If the mark is extremely well known like LEGO, then the common field of endeavour may well be drawn more widely than for an obscure mark.

A problem common to unregistered and registered marks is that when the allegedly damaging act is examined it may be found that it is a legitimate competitive activity. The desire not to hamper competitive trade has a strong influence on the attitudes of the judges when they apply the law. Since in the UK there is no specific unfair trade practices legislation, many industrial property disputes are attempts to halt unfair trading and it falls to the judges to define in detail what is legitimate competition and what is not.

These aspects of passing off are best understood by means of the following examples, which are by no means comprehensive.

In the **Lego** case (9), the plaintiff was the world famous manufacturer of coloured plastic construction bricks for children. The defendant's product, also called "Lego", was coloured plastic irrigation pipes and garden equipment. This firm was long established, trading in many other countries without dispute. They now wanted to expand into Britain but the plaintiff argued that after long exposure to Lego bricks the public would think that the plastic pipes were manufactured by their firm. A survey of opinion was carried out among the general public and seemed to support this view. The report of this case in the High Court includes a detailed discussion of the administration of such surveys and their efficiency. The House of Lords decided that confusion was extremely likely since the pipes would be made of the same type of brightly coloured plastics as the bricks. Therefore use of the name "Lego" was forbidden for the pipes. A major factor in this decision was the designation of a field of activity, working in coloured plastics, which included the essence of both companies' endeavours.

Another type of case occurs where a group of firms use a name in common according to certain rules as with certification trade marks. They can then challenge attempts to use the name outside the rules. The case involving Champagne is an example, only when grapes from a specific area in France are used can the product be called "Champagne" (10).

In the case of **Annabel's v Schock**(11) the issue turned on common field of activity. A night club and an escort agency were both considered to be in night time entertainment and therefore confusion was possible between the two. In the two cases involving common activities considered so far, the result was in favour of the complainant. The difficulty for the courts is to estimate the type of connections between businesses that the public is likely to make. On the whole the analogies are drawn generously. The one area where categories seem to be drawn rather narrowly and claims discouraged is that of character merchandising.

The recent history of character merchandising started with the **Uncle Mac** case of 1947 (12). McCulloch, better known as "Uncle Mac" was a famous children's radio broadcaster. A breakfast cereal was brought out and publicised as Uncle Mac's puffed wheat. The broadcaster failed to prevent this unauthorised use of his radio name as it was held that the presentation of children's programmes had nothing in common with the manufacture of cereals.

Similarly in 1975 the author of books about the **Wombles,** little creatures which picked up rubbish and lived on Wimbledon Common, was unable to prevent a firm renting out skips (large rubbish bins) from calling itself "Wombles Skips Ltd" (13).

There are a large number of cases following this general rule in the area of entertainment and exploitation of individuals and invented characters. Where the inventor of the characters exercises some form of quality control over a range of products such as soft toys, then rights are established. This was illustrated in an Australian case involving **Sesame Street** characters (14). The Australian Broadcasting corporation had Sesame Street characters made and sold under licence and managed to fend off imitators. It had a direct interest in the field of soft toy reproductions, because it used its licences to exert quality control over the toys marketed under its name.

One final example is the **Pub Squash** case (15). This is an Australian case but was finally decided by the Privy Council in London. Two brands of lemon squash were sold in similarly styled but distinguishable cans backed up by intense TV advertising which was on identical themes elaborated in a similar fashion: strong men indulging in sports, then drinking from the can with a voice-over proclaiming the pleasures of real old-fashioned squash. It was held that the defendants were taking advantage of the successful packaging and advertising of the plaintiff's drink, but that this was a normal competitive practice and had to be tolerated. It was very much a borderline case and generated great interest.

It is clear from these examples how general principles are elaborated through case law to show how particular situations should be interpreted. In intellectual property, the various common law countries have sufficiently similar systems that case law is interchangeable between them although not binding when it stems from foreign jurisdictions. The countries involved are the UK and USA, Canada, Australia and New Zealand. The UK is having to some extent to move out of this state of unity to approximate more closely to the legal traditions of continental Europe. Our membership of the EEC and the European Patent and Trade Mark conventions obliges us to strive for legal systems common in their effect even though different in their mode of operation. We do not need to change the system but we do need to modify our interpretations.

Chapter 3   International Protection   of Trade Marks

3.1   The Paris Convention, 1883

This Convention covers registered trade marks and the law of unfair competition, as well as patents and designs. There is a six month period running from the date of the initial application during which registration for the same mark can be made in other countries. The two main principles of the Convention are as follows.

1. **The right to equal treatment.** This asserts that foreign applicants and owners of trade marks have to be treated in the same way as domestic applicants and owners.

2. **The right to priority within a six month period.** During these six months, any application will be backdated to the date of initial application. As there is no novelty requirement for trade marks, this is important only if another applicant applies for the same or a very similar mark during that six month period.

3.2   An EEC Trade Mark

This is not yet available but the planning for it is well advanced. There is to be a European Trade Mark Office and a single registration will provide protection in all EEC countries (16).

On application, a search will be made through the Registers of all the countries. A word will have to satisfy the requirements of being distinctive but not descriptive and also not misleading or obscene, a place name or surname, and any other restrictions, in all the community languages. It remains to be seen how much this will restrict the availability of words.

In the UK, the holder of a non-registered but established mark can object to registration of a mark which would be misleadingly similar to it. Our continental European partners have usually ruled that only the owners of other registered marks can object in this way. This has been a matter of dispute between Britain and Ireland, the only two common law countries, and the rest of the EEC. It is likely that only registered marks will be counted. This reflects the desire for certainty in the Registry. If non- registered marks can be relied upon, then the applicants cannot be sure at any time of having met all objections.

Chapter 4   Trade Mark Documentation

In Britain as in other countries the Trade Mark Registry provides the means of searching the Official Register. In addition there are some commercial services in existence. The services available in the UK will be described.

4.1   Official Services

These are based on the Trade Mark registry in London, which is housed jointly with the Patent Office (17).

a) Official Journal (Trade Marks)

This Journal, normally referred to as OJ(TM), is the sister of the Patent Office's patents journal, the OJ(P). Each week it lists and illustrates marks accepted by the Registry. Occasionally a mark is listed prior to acceptance for comments as to its distinctiveness or any other characteristcs. The OJ is useful only for current awareness as volumes are not cumulated.

The SRIS holds a complete set of these Journals plus a name index to trade mark applicants and holders. Unfortunately this is out of date, going back to 1978 only.

b) The Trade Mark Registry

If a TM number is known, one can check the Register to find out whether it has lapsed or is still in force and when the next renewal fees are due. Details of the proprietor, assignees and registered users are available from the Register entry as are descriptions of any disclaimers or other conditions imposed upon a mark.

The Registry also has a public search room where various indexes are available for novelty searching. These are grouped according to the thirty-four divisions of the classification of goods plus another eight divisions for services. The entry for each TM consists of the words and symbols which make it up and also gives details of the owner. They are cut from the OJ(TM) and mounted in loose leaf files; one searches simply by going through these files. There are separate files for pending TMs and for marks prior to 1938. These have to be searched separately since the classification of goods was changed at the same time as the new Act was introduced, and the backlog was never reclassified.

There is a separate index consisting of a list of word-stems upon which different prefixes and suffixes could hang. These need to be searched, because a word could be refused registration if it sounds similar to another when spoken.

Other separate indexes consist of shapes and symbols.

The system is cumbersome and difficult to use. Since charging is by time spent searching, haste may lead to confusion. Searching is entirely manual at present but the Registry is in the process of being computerised as part of the efficiency improvements agreed for the entire industrial property administration.

Online searching

A plan to computerise the Register and the searching facilities has been formulated and is proceeding. This stems in part from the Rayner efficiency reviews of the civil service which recommend that money be made available for computerisation. The intention is that thirty terminals should be available in a new public area on the ground floor of State House. However, this can be only a temporary measure as State House is only a temporary home. Tenders have been put out and some contracts agreed, but it is not yet known when the system will become operational (18).

The system is designed to provide either an

automatic search for a mark or to allow browsing to look for prefixes either in the whole file or in particular classes. These would be displayed as a list of marks with classes and a list of applicable goods from within those classes. The searcher then chooses these marks for which he requires full details.

4.2   Commercial Searching

Trade mark agents will do some searching, but they regard it as best left to the Registry when an application is made.

Freelance literature and patent searchers also undertake trade mark searches but, unless they do this quite often, they do not gain any particular degree of expertise.

There exist a number of specific search services. These are online and cover a number of European countries and the USA. Either an individual can carry out his own search or the organisation will do it for him possibly offering additional consultants' services. Words and numbers can be searched as on any online system, and symbols can also be searched using a special classification of shapes.

UKTM

In 1986 Pergamon Infoline opened a commercial online database of UK trade marks called simply UKTM. It is similar to and will be in direct competition with the official online service. Being available on the public telephone network and on a large host is itself an advantage over the official service (19). This service has attracted very heavy usage, but it is still too soon to tell if such use levels will be maintained.

Compumark

This is an old and well established service. It is based in Antwerp, Belgium and is a collection on computer of the RTMs of some 16 countries. The organisation also carries out manual searches for other countries acting as an information broker.

Names of proprietors can be sought, as well as

words, figures and shapes of marks. Specific services offered are:

novelty searching: searching for a specific name and symbol or one that looks and/or sounds similar.

marking service: matching the register to pick up any mark similar to a given mark that is entered.

current awareness: new marks as they appear.

creation service: making up a TM built round essential elements specified by the client.

Staff will also identify case law covering particular situations.

Duplicates of the database on punched cards are sold to the public.

Trade Mark Scan

This service covers US trade marks only and is available from Derwent. The Derwent organisation mainly deals in patent information and has been described in detail in the patents chapters. Trade Mark Scan stands apart from the patent services. It gives an automatic search and also a means to browse. However, the search logic is not known which makes it difficult to plan a more effective search. Basically one enters a word and it finds the same and similar ones (eg "skeeta" for mosquito). For browsing, full details must be printed out which makes the service expensive and also unsatisfactory since many pages of data are generated which then have to be edited.

National Registers

Each country maintains its own national Register of trade marks. Some of these are still on paper but most have by now been computerised. Compu Mark is the one organisation that has collated these Registers. If a search in a particular country is required, a local freelance searcher or trade mark agent can usually be found to do it. Official registers are not readily obtainable outside the jurisdiction to which they refer.

Pharmaceutical Trade Mark Directory

This is a unique database which operates only for the pharmaceutical industry(20). It is mounted by Intercontinental Medical Statistics Ltd which has a well established reputation for producing reliable market surveys of products and countries. It is a directory of use rather than of registrations and therefore contains non-registered marks as well as registered ones.

A "typical" user of the Directory could be a company which is using a name to sell a product in a certain country for a certain length of time. It could also be researching companies in a field it wishes to move into.
a) It may be concerned that the same or a similar name is being used by a second company for a similar product. This could be an act of piracy but on the other hand might be revealing an unexpected commercial relationship.
b) If a name has been used and then no longer appears, appropriate legal steps can be taken.

Linkups with clinical trial and product registration dossiers are being considered. Expansion to include related fields of activity is also under investigation. Veterinary medicaments are covered but there are other fields which are not, such as chemicals, cosmetics, agrichemicals, foods and surgical apparatus.

This is a valuable service to businesses but it only covers a narrow field because this is where the company's expertise lies. Such a service must be reliable to be of any use and it takes time for a company to build up a sufficient reputation. For this reason it would probably not be possible to have a similar database covering all technologies at once. These systems are inherently specialised.

InterBrand

This is not a searching service. It offers a computer-aided trade mark creation system. It is an international company with offices in London, New York, Tokyo and Frankfurt. Other trade mark creation services exist on both sides of the Atlantic, but none is particularly well known.

SECTION 5   RELATED LEGISLATION

Within intellectual property law there are some topics which fit uncomfortably in the standard categories of protectability. Thus there is some argument as to how they should be treated, with different approaches being taken in different countries. Of this type we will examine:

    1.   living organisms, and
    2.   computer software and hardware.

There are also topics covered by laws which cannot be categorised as intellectual property laws, but which have an at-times substantial impact upon the manner in which intellectual property is exploited or protected. In this context we will examine:

    3.   confidential information,
    4.   data protection,
    5.   counterfeiting, and
    6.   the Trades Description Acts.

Chapter 1   Living Organisms

The protection of newly created organisms belongs partly to patent law and partly to special breeders' rules.

Micro Organisms

It has always been a principle that naturally occurring phenomena cannot constitute inventions. This principle should include all living things since we cannot create life out of inanimate matter. Nevertheless, micro organisms have become big business. They are "made" through genetic engineering, and also through the cultivation of a purified strain taken out of a naturally occurring mixed colony such as occurs in the soil or in liquids. Somehow, because the interference of man is required for the creation and single-strain reproduction of these organisms, they have been allowed as inventions and may be patented as such (1). See Section 2, 4.1.1 under criteria for patentability for further details of their protection.

Reproducibility

A problem with patenting living matter is that a reader of the specification cannot easily set about reproducing the invention. Genetic engineering patents take a known organism and manipulate it using known laboratory techniques. If the starting organism is readily identifiable and available, then such an invention might be reproducible. When an invention consists of taking an organism out of the soil and purifying its strain, then it is definitely not reproducible since the original organism is not obtainable. If it were, there would be no invention. To overcome this problem of inadequate disclosure, many national patent acts have inserted a requirement that a sample of the organism is to be deposited in a recognised culture collection where it can be maintained in a reservoir. Once the patent is granted, then any member of the public can receive a sample from this deposit.

There has been much discussion as to whether the sample should be freely available from the date the application is published or the date the patent is granted. In the USA the question does not arise as the two dates are identical, but is important in any country with an early publication system. Availability of the organism gives an enquirer a far greater advantage than does the availability of a specification alone, and this advantage may be felt to be unfair when protection is by no means guaranteed. Therefore in Britain and in the European Patent Convention the date of availability is now set as the date of grant (2).

Each country specifies its own list of approved culture collections and, initially, it was necessary for a patentee to have to make multiple deposits to satisfy various countries. Therefore a special convention was signed, the **Budapest Treaty** of 1977, to be administered by WIPO (3). Under this Treaty, any member state can nominate one or more of its national culture collections to be international depositaries. It does this by certifying that conditions of the Treaty are fulfilled and will continue to be so in the future. All signatories agree to accept a deposit in any international depository as being sufficient for their national law. As of July first 1984, fifteen states were party to this Treaty as also is the European Patent Office.

These collections are normally housed in large biological institutes or in universities and contain a great deal of material most of which has nothing to do with patents. They are rather imperfect organisations. In a piece of research carried out in 1978, Bannister found that catalogues were often out of date and it was difficult to locate the required specimen(4). These are really administrative problems: in UK law and also in that of most other countries, the culture collection address and the number of the deposit are supposed to be published in the specification. If the sample is no longer available, then the applicant or patentee is required to supply another. However some collection administrators were unclear as to when and to whom they could make samples available. Present cuts in funding in Britain may well have an adverse effect on the administration of such collections. At the same time they are very vulnerable to power cuts and natural disasters in rich as well as in poor countries (5). For these reasons it may well turn out that the result of the Budapest Treaty to create only one reservoir of an organism to serve all users is a bad one. At least two should be available to guard against accidents.

Higher Animals

New species are created by selective breeding programmes. These do not qualify as inventions and are specifically excluded from patentable subject matter in the 1977 Patents Act in the United Kingdom. Animals are not allowed to be patented in any country. However, this prohibition applies only to animals as the essence of the invention. Where an animal is important in operating an invention, but is not the invention itself, it might very occasionally become patentable. For instance in West Germany in patent no 2935634 applied for in 1979, a rodent was patented as a vehicle for the testing of a certain vaccine. It had unique metabolic properties and only this one animal species could be used. This was a patent for a new use of a known species. The patent was allowed for testing the vaccine specifying the rodent as the testing apparatus.

Higher Plants

The USA allows patents for plants which have been specially bred. There is a separate plant patent sequence. The plant, and its fruit or seeds or any other characteristic and important part, is described in great detail, often with coloured photographs. Full protection of the plant in all aspects ensues. The availability of the plant through seeds is controlled separately from the Budapest Treaty, which is for micro organisms only.

These patents are unique to the USA. Many other countries including the USA have evolved a parallel special protection simply for the reproductive parts to control the marketing of seeds or bulbs. The living plant and its fruit and or flowers are not protected. It is the seeds that are normally of most concern and these are protected. There is an International Convention for the protection of new varieties of plants. It is known as UPOV and shares its secretary-general and administration with WIPO. UPOV is opposed to dual protection of plants, it specifies either breeders' rights or patents, but not both.

In Britain the relevant legislation is the **Plant Varieties and Seeds Act 1964.** This provides for three years of growing trials supervised by the Ministry of Agriculture to ensure that the variety breeds true. Then it is given a name and placed with other plants of the same type. The Ministry of Agriculture makes regulations afresh for each type of plant and these will differ according to their trading patterns. This Act was revised but not substantially changed in 1984. It grants the owner exclusive rights over the distribution and sale of seeds, bulbs or other reproductive parts of the plant. Plants for which protection has been granted include crops such as cereals, fruit trees and potatoes and ornamental plants like roses and chrysanthemums (6).

Chapter 2   Computer Software and Hardware

Computers operate by means of complex mechanisms which embody sophisticated concepts. Both the concepts and their execution fit partly into copyright law and partly into patent law. The hardware is machinery. A new type of computer, an arrangement of electrical components which carry out certain functions, is readily patentable (7). Computer programs, the software, present difficulties both of definition and of categorisation (8).

Patent law does not allow the patenting of instructions; indeed it excludes computer programs explicitly in many countries including the UK. If, therefore, a computer program is to come within the scope of patent law, there has to be an actual connection between the program and a product or process. A computer program treated as part of a mechanism can be patented.

The usual treatment of a program is to regard it as a piece of written text under copyright law. This is allowed for in the British Copyright Act. The text might be meaningless at a casual glance, but to an informed reader its content is clear and informative. Copyright ensues as soon as the program is embodied in a permanent form. This can be as code inside a computer even when there is no printed version (9).

Two particular problems arise with this copyright approach. First of all, computer programs fall within two categories. There are "high level" languages which tend to read as a highly formalised version of English. Programmers write in these languages as they are designed to approximate human manipulations. However the computer operates using a very basic language in which the "words" are usually represented as combinations of the binary digits 0 and 1. These digits are represented physically as the closed and open positions of switches. Each computer has its own "machine code" and a "compiler" translates the high level languages into this machine code. Running the program on the computer consists of setting the appropriate switches to be on and off so that electric current runs in certain patterns through the machine.

It has been argued that high level languages can count as text for copyright purposes but that machine code which is reproduced in the circuitry of the computer is entirely physical apparatus and beyond the scope of copyright protection. This argument has generally been rejected : machine code has an unambiguous meaning coded by its binary digits and therefore qualifies as a language(10).

The second problem is concerned with different versions of high level languages. The same operations, carried out in different languages, may appear entirely different in those languages. This has been regarded simply as translation. But sometimes operations in one language do not exist in another. The logical structure is so different that, although the same end result may be achieved, the sequence of operations is changed. It is the rule in copyright that it is not an idea which is protected, but the manner of its expression. Is the treatment of these diverse languages as mere translations tantamount to taking the idea? If so, this could greatly hamper normal progress in software development. It could possibly be treated as being akin to writing a film script from a novel or to composing a musical arrangement for quite different instruments from those originally scored. The originator must give permission, but the finished product has a separate copyright (11).

Legislation

The UK

In the Patents Act 1977, following the European Patent Convention, patents for computer programs are specifically included but, as with the medical treatment area, programs are only excluded per se. Therefore the situation is not greatly different from that under the 1949 Act, under which programs were allowed but plain mathematical methods not. It is possible under the new Act, as under the old, to devise formulations which allow a patent to be granted for what is essentially a program by emphasising the function. For example a patent was granted for the program behind CAIRS, the information retrieval package devised at the Food Industries Research Association at Leatherhead (12). It was presented as a means for storing information at higher densities therefore getting more into a smaller space. Strangely enough the patent covers a computer program and a means for presenting information, both of which are inherently unpatentable!

Under the Copyright Act 1956, computer programs were not mentioned explicitly. That could hardly have been expected, since computing was still in its infancy. However, as the Act was drafted enumeratively with protected categories listed in fair detail, the extent of implicit protection is unclear. Programs were, however, implicitly covered under the general protection for any text fixed in permanent form. But the industry indicated that it felt uncertain and unprotected and would not wish to incur the expense of a test case. While a new Copyright Act is awaited, an interim extension has been enacted in 1985, declaring specifically that computer programs are to be treated as literary works and that versions in different languages are to be regarded as translations (13). This ensures programs the full protection given to literature. One great advantage is that "computer program" itself is not defined. On the assumption that anything at the time accepted by the industry as being a program will be regarded as such, there will henceforth be scope for technical development. The 1986 White Paper confirms (14) that this amendment will be incorporated into the new Act as it stands with a few additions to clarify the scope of protection.

One disadvantage in a fast developing highly competitive industry like computing is that there is no register, and therefore no record kept of programs and their owners. It is very difficult to trace the owners in these circumstances, particularly considering the high turnover in firms and personnel. Tracing of owners is of course essential if one program is required for modification by another programmer. This is how much progress occurs, but terms for licensing or collaboration need to be negotiated first. The easier it is to locate the owner, the less the temptation to just pirate the copy. Protection without formalities is of course a great advantage, as is the international protection provided by membership of the appropriate Conventions. They arise automatically upon creation of a work while formalities cost time and money. Therefore, as owners, the industry supports automatic copyright protection although it is arguable that their best interests lie in a register.

The USA

As in Europe, patents are generally not available for software products.

When the Copyright Act of 1976 came into force, computer programs were assumed to be protected as literary works. A residual committee, CONTU, looked at the effects of new technology on copyright (15). Following its recommendations a definition of computer programs was incorporated into the Act: a set of statements or instructions to be used directly or indirectly in a computer in order to bring about a certain result. Programs are from that time on protected explicitly. The most interesting relevant case is the **Apple Computers** case, 1982 (16). In the court of first instance it was ruled that a distinction should be made between application programs which create results for a human audience, and operating programs which simply govern other programs. This was overturned by the Court of Appeal which ruled that all programs are equal under the law so far as protection is concerned.

The same general principles of translation from one type of program to another also apply as in the UK. The first judgment in an infringement case that did not involve direct and virtually identical copying was given in 1975 in the US in the case of **Whelan v Jaslow Dental Laboratory.** The Federal trial court held that the version in Basic did infringe the version in Event Driven

Language, (EDL), even though simple translation did not take place because of the dissimilar structure of the languages. The Court reasoned that, by studying the flow of information and the required operations in one language, "manner of operation" was copied in the other. Also the screens of information produced were almost identical in format and terminology and finally visitors at all trade shows thought there was no substantial difference.

The above decision appears to be the correct one for the industry and yet it seems to be taking the idea rather than the expression. This is the point at which copyright concepts are least adequate to cope with the complexity of actual practice.

In one area the US has modified copyright law and produced a completely new Act tailor-made for a piece of technology. This is the **Semiconductor Chip Protection Act 1984** (18). It is a unique piece of legislation which protects the templates from which chips are made by photographic reduction and etching and various other processes. The starting point for this process is the circuit diagram which is to be drawn on to the chip. The design is registered with the Copyright Office. There is no examination for novelty, but the issue of invalidity on grounds of lack of novelty can be raised later. The design, called a **mask work**, must be registered within two years of the date of first commercial exploitation if this is within the US or another country which gives reciprocal protection, or if the owner is a national of one of those countries. The owner of the mask work then has exclusive rights over reproduction and distribution of the work and products embodying it. There is no right over use. Protection lasts for ten years.

This Act is a hybrid between patent and copyright laws. Function and design are considered to establish novelty as in a patent but there is no examination, just registration as with a US copyright. The exclusive rights are narrowly drawn. The advantage of creating a new type of industrial property is that it will be tailor made to fit the exact requirements. As a disadvantage, the ease of use of the international conventions is lost and there will be an inevitable lack of familiarity with the precise provisions which could harden into resistance if more "customised" Acts were created to deal with unfamiliar technology. The reciprocity requirement in this particular instance has lead to other countries examining their provisions for mask works. In the UK for instance they are protected as artistic works being etchings derived from original drawings. WIPO is looking into a treaty on integrated circuits.

Australia

This country is included because a number of important cases have arisen there, and because its law has diverged from its original UK base. An era has drawn to a close now that all remaining legal ties between Australia and Britain have been cut. Australian law is bound to take a divergent path with no more Privy Council appeals to impose conformity with UK decisions.

Patents have played no role in software protection in Australia. The emphasis has been on copyright law. The most significant case has been that of **Apple Computers** involving the same software as the US Apple case. It was ruled by the Federal Court of Appeal that operating systems programs written in high level languages are literary works and that the machine code version is an adaptation and is likewise protected. However this was only after the court of first instance caused a furore by ruling that computer programs being unreadable by humans were non literary by definition. This view offered no protection at all and was promptly overruled. However, the debate is by no means concluded on this issue as the decision was subsequently re-reversed and may require yet more elucidation (19).

Databases

The discussion so far has been about computer programs in the abstract, irrespective of their content. A computer held database of information will carry a copyright by virtue of being a compilation of information. It may already be in copyright by virtue of a parallel printed version.

There is no case law, but the question has been asked: who owns the copyright in the search output? The database owner usually considers the copyright remains with him and normally pre-empts the issue by specifying control in the contract a user signs before searching. However, since the searcher devotes skill and labour to extracting the information, it seems plausible that this copyright should belong to the searcher.

Extra-legal protection

Just as the copyright issue for database searching is pre-empted by use of contracts to regulate the use of output, so is legal control of software to some extent overshadowed by extra legal forms of protection (20).

For mainframe and mini computers, programs are often complex and are perfected only after many months of work. When bought legally, the suppliers will usually offer detailed documentation and an after-care service in case of faults; or an offer may be made to carry out modifications and graft on further packages. A pirate copy would have no backup services. These services are sufficiently valuable for their provision to deter use of pirate software.

Secondly there are various spoilers and codes which act as keys to prevent unauthorised access to a program or at least prevent copying once access is gained.

Both these techniques provide much more effective protection than copyright law for larger computers and their software. A survey by Elsom in 1981 showed that these manufacturers do not worry about piracy. The problem lies in the booming market for micros where short-run very specialised programs are written. Even games which have a high sales volume are vulnerable as the sales runs are quite short. The problem is that it is too expensive to provide documentation or electronic keys at this level. The problem remains one of enforcement. Tough penalties applied frequently enough are a deterrent, but piracy is insidious and hard to detect. This will be further described under counterfeiting. For micros, a number of successful companies have concentrated on selling a short-run edition of a program and moving on to another one. Any further use of software, even if unauthorised, is welcomed as providing publicity for their products. The user might buy an authorised version of the next program. This strategy works particularly well for games. It makes a virtue of necessity, treats the customer as a friend rather than an enemy and diverts corporate energies away from enforcement towards creation and promotion of their products (21).

This area is only partially regulated by statute.
Since one has usually to rely on case law to
establish a right, the extent of protection tends
to remain restricted, the rights allowed being to
some extent at the mercy of prevailing judicial
attitudes.

Although patents and designs are awarded for the
development of new processes and products, often
there are parts of the development which are kept
secret and called "know how". One can have know
how agreements together with or separate from
product licence agreements. Very often entire
development programs are kept secret. Such trade
secrets are targets for industrial espionage or
other means of discovery.

English law does not protect information as such.
Protection does not depend upon the actual content
of documents, but upon the establishment of a
confidential relationship. Once such confidence
has been imposed, the law will assist in
maintaining it whether the information concerns
the intimacies of a marital relationship or the
construction of a new factory.

The major authority in defining a confidential
relationship is the case of **Coco v Clark** (22). In
that case it was held that there are three
necessary components of a successful breach of
confidence action:

a)   that the information is of a confidential
      nature,
b)   that the information was communicated in
      circumstances which implied an obligation of
      confidence, and

c)   that unauthorised use was made of the
     information.
There is a rich case law which indicates when
information is of a confidential nature and what
circumstances imply confidence(23).

Public Interest in the Information

Commercial confidence is a convenient barrier to
the disclosure of much information required by
consumer groups. Information is also required by
members of the public living close to certain
types of factory or subject to pollution of
various kinds. Hazards are usually declared by
public authorities to be non-existent but the
quality of evidence is never made available to
those likely to be affected by it so that they can
assess the data for themselves. (Hence the present
public distrust of "experts" and of science and
technology in general). The British Campaign for
Freedom of Information is trying to ensure greater
availability of important data (24).

Confidentiality law does admit a public interest
defence. It is a rather limited provision but has
recently been allowed to expand as can be seen in
the following sequence of cases.

In the case of the **Crossman diaries** (25),which
decided whether details of an ex-Cabinet
Minister's life could be published, there was a
public interest in their publication. It was
argued for the Government that there was also a
public interest in collective responsibility for
cabinet decisions and that the publication of
individual views would harm this by inhibiting the
open expression of opinion in cabinet meetings.
The volume in dispute concerned discussions that
were ten years and three general elections out of
date, and it was held that public memory of
collective decisions would not go back that far.
Therefore in this case the interest in publication
was allowed to take precedence.

In contrast to this, in cases concerning safety of
drugs where the information is of immediate
importance, the interest in protecting potential
victims is frequently not allowed to outweigh the
commercial rights of the producing companies. The
best known case in this category is that involving
the drug Thalidomide (26). The Sunday Times

newspaper only got permission to publish details of the tragedy by going to the European Court of Human Rights.

The Thalidomide case was somewhat atypical, but there have been others. A TV programme on the drug "Primodos" which was alleged to deform babies (in a similar fashion to thalidomide), was prevented from being shown (27). Internal information was used, it is almost inevitable that the information will first come from inside a company as only they have all the data but will not allow inspection. By its nature the causal link is a possiblity rather than a proven certainty and there is a clear interest for those at risk to be able to assess the dangers for themselves. The court took the attitude that as the information was generated internally there was an obligation of confidence. When faced with this attitude the public interest defence is a very weak one due to the weight given to the relationship and the relative lack of interest in the actual information.

However, the legal climate has changed since then and these cases may well be decided the other way if they came to court today. Some recent judgments show a pendulum swing in judicial attitudes. Indiscriminate disclosure to the press is not encouraged but, depending on the type and degree of iniquity, disclosure is permissible if made to an appropriate body. In a case involving police corruption this was accepted as being the press. When jockey club rules were broken with some associated minor crime it was felt appropriate to notify the jockey club and the police. Public interest can also attach to news of events other than iniquities. In the case of **Lion Laboratories v Evans**, newspapers wished to publish details of inaccuracies in a new type of breathalyser the police were introducing. The manufacturer did not want this unreliability known and argued that, as the proposed disclosure would not reveal any iniquity in the form of an unlawful act carried out by it, there could be no public interest in disclosure. Publication was nevertheless allowed as the public interest was agreed to include justice being seen to be done. This new attitude approaches a freedom of information ethic and is an example of how the law does adjust in line with public mores (28).

Stolen Information

Information is sometimes taken not in a relationship of confidence but by straightforward "theft". A piece of paper may be physically stolen or an employee might be pursuaded with money or the promise of a new job to tell a competitor the latest plans. Industrial espionage is very sophisticated and can also involve hidden microphones, powerful cameras and any other "bugging" devices available (29).

Information cannot be "stolen" in the sense of the criminal law because theft is defined as an event which permanently deprives the owner of his property. Money or an object can only be held by one person at a time. However, I can share information with other people and then they have the information and so do I. Therefore, information taken is not lost at its source and can not be stolen. In the absence of an effective criminal deterrent, an aggrieved owner of information must try to use the civil law to protect his interests (30).

The law of confidential information does not deal with this situation. As explained above, the law deals with a confidential relationship, but there is no obligation of confidence upon a thief. In the case of a disloyal employee one can use the Prevention of Corruption Act if he is paid for the knowledge transferred. Espionage by an outsider seems in general to break no law at all.

This is rather makeshift and unsatisfactory. The **Law Commission** in 1983 published a Report examining the entire area of confidential and stolen information (31). They proposed formalising much of the existing case law as a new statutory "tort". A tort is a generalised civil wrong done to one or more members of a wide class of people towards whom a duty is owed. The best known example is negligence; one owes a duty of care towards fellow citizens in a variety of circumstances and, if this is not discharged, a victim can sue for negligence. In the same way, it was proposed, there should be a duty to respect confidence in all circumstances where a reasonable person would understand that confidence was implied. This formalises the **Coco v Clark** definition of a relationship of confidence. By setting it into the well developed body of tort law, remedies and scope of application are well defined and one's rights would be more certain.

In addition it was proposed to impose an implied duty of confidence in cases where information is stolen so that these too could be treated as actions for breach of confidence. Unfortunately there has been no Government response to the Report as yet and it appears to have been shelved.

The Potential of a Breach of Confidence Action

To illustrate the usefulness of a civil equivalent of theft a most unusual example is the Australian case of **Franklin v Giddins** in 1978 (32). The plaintiffs grew nectarines commercially and developed a unique strain by cross breeding with peaches. The defendant was a friend who helped pick the fruit and learned how to propagate the stock. When he acquired his own orchard, the defendant stole some cuttings at night and was soon growing the same variety of nectarines. If he had been charged with theft this would have resulted in a fine or possibly a prison sentence. The plaintiffs, however, wanted the competition to cease, so they brought an action for breach of confidence in that he stole the genetic information defining the strain. There was no confidential relationship but, because of his unconscionable conduct, one was imposed. In this particular civil action it was permissible as a remedy to have all the trees destroyed when the defendant was found guilty.

Chapter 4   Data Protection

This covers the rights of individuals to inspect personal data concerning themselves in order to know what is being held and to correct it if there are any errors. There is no question of any property right in the data, it is more a civil liberties issue.

Various countries have passed data protection legislation during the past decade as the increasing use of computers has meant that not only is more information being held, but that it is probably more accessible and also more easily linked to other types of information (33).

In the United Kingdom the Data Protection Act 1984 (34) established a statutory framework for the regulation of the electronic storage and retrieval of personal data. This framework is administered by the Registrar of data protection, who commenced registration of holders of personal data on a computer in November 1985. Under the Act, data subjects are entitled to inspect records referring to themselves and have them altered if they contain errors. Rights of inspection and alteration only come into force in November 1987.

The Registrar, with a staff of around 20 people, is to police the users. Changes in format of records can be required and individual complaints will be investigated. The users have to follow eight principles which cover basically good housekeeping practice. These are as follows.

1)   Personal data held by users is to be processed fairly and lawfully;

2) It is to be held only for one or more specified purposes;

3) It is not to be used or disclosed in a manner incompatible with those purposes;

4) It is to be adequate, relevant and not excessive;

5) It is to be accurate and kept up to date; and

6) It is not to be held for longer than necessary.

7) Individuals have the right to be informed if information is held on them, to have access to their own records and to correct them where appropriate.

8) Security measures will be taken against the accidental loss or destruction of, or the unauthorised disclosure, alteration or destruction of data.

This final principle also applies to operators of computer bureaux.

The effectiveness of the Registrar is rather questionable given that he has only a small staff, but the Act is at least in principle a useful corrective to excessive surveillance. There are, however, two serious flaws:

1. The Act applies only to files held on computer. Any sensitive data needs merely to be transferred to paper to be safe from detection.

2. Files held in the interest of the state covering national security, detection of crime and several other categories are exempt.

The activities of the police and security services in holding vast numbers of files, full of gossip and erroneous and misconceived information, is a major area of concern. Periodic revelations of previously unrecognised areas of life kept under surveillance by MI5, such as the appointment of BBC journalists, is not reassuring.

However, the Act's existence gives a focal point
for pressure groups. It is a step towards freedom
to have the right to know that a file does exist.
Secret surveillance can only breed mistrust. It is
possible that the Act could be extended if it is
seen to be working well. It is too early to judge
that yet.

Chapter 5   Counterfeiting

Counterfeiting is a very broad problem. It is the copying of the appearance of a well known product so that a (usually cheaper) substitute is bought instead, the purchaser thinking that he is acquiring the well known article. Perfumes, car components, cassettes for audio and video tapes, cans of drink and even medicines are examples of counterfeitable goods.

Trade marks are copied and copyrights of pictures on the outsides of products are infringed. In general everything is done to make the product look like something well known and then put a cheap and nasty substitute in place of the product (35).

Much damage is done: non-functioning machinery is an obvious case as are bogus drugs and agricultural products. Sometimes the substituted product is of reasonably good quality and a company is merely increasing its profits by using someone else's reputation. Even this is damaging to a company which has invested a lot of money in establishing its name.

The problem here is one of enforcement. Laws must be made as easy as possible to apply, and penalties have to be severe enough for it to be worth the effort of catching offenders and to be a deterrent to them. For example when unlimited fines or two years' imprisonment became the penalties for audio and video piracy in 1983, the conviction rate sharply increased. The previous fine of £50 or two months in prison was too slight a deterrent to be worth the time and expense of preparing a case for prosecution.

Counterfeiting

The enforcement problem is an international one as the pirates and counterfeiters conduct thriving import and export businesses especially around the EEC where strict control of distribution channels is not allowed.

In many respects the problem of political will to enforce anti-piracy measures is also one of rich countries v poor countries. Thriving sales of cheap counterfeit goods can be a great boost to a youthful economy. Only when there is enough productive work to ensure continuing prosperity can considerations of respectability come into play to encourage vigorous enforcement.

Chapter 6   The Trades Description Acts 1968-72

These Acts are of general application to goods and
define a criminal offence of making a "false trade
description". The definition is a very wide one
and covers performance and characteristics of
items, testing and approval of their functions and
past history. Any indication of these matters,
whether direct or indirect, will fall under the
Acts (36).

A description can be applied in almost any manner
including orally or in advertisements. Most
commonly a description will be in writing and
attached to the item.

An offence is committed if the trade description
is false. This means broadly that the public must
be likely to be misled by this description into
purchasing the goods.

Similar provisions in the Acts deal with services
and accommodation. In particular false
descriptions of holidays and holiday accommodation
have been suppressed after a number of successful
prosecutions. The Acts also cover unfair tags
indicating price reductions for goods which were
never sold at the higher price, or which attribute
British origin to imported goods.

As a means of protecting individual traders
against unfair competition, the criminal law is
never as effective as the civil law. The standard
of proof for a criminal prosecution is much higher
than the balance of probabilities required in a
civil action. There will be no injunction to stop
further activities, or award of damages to the
injured party, only a fine.

Thus the main application of these Acts is in the wider public sphere of consumer protection where there is a public interest in ensuring good practice, but no single consumer is sufficiently injured to make bringing an individual action worth while. Enforcement is in the hands of local trading standards authorities. They receive complaints from the public and can also act on their own initiative. They obtain evidence by making test purchases and by entering premises to seize goods and documents. They are under the control of the Board of Trade for purposes of overall policy and co-ordination, for instance to prevent multiple small prosecutions against one defendant.

SECTION 6 EEC COMPETITION LAW

As was mentioned in Section 1, Chapter 4, intellectual property sits uneasily in the framework of the EEC's competition policy. It is allowed to exist, and full rights can be exercised in relation to non-EEC countries; on the other hand, much case law has been developed to delineate the essential rights of intellectual property which can be exercised and those which, by preserving national boundaries within the EEC, cannot be permitted.

A number of Articles of the Treaty define the ethos of free competition (1). These provisions only affect activities on a scale large enough to influence trade between member states.

Article 85 prohibits agreements between undertakings which could prevent, restrict or distort competition. However, some exemptions are granted where benefit is presumed to exist or can be demonstrated.

Article 86 prohibits the abuse of a dominant position by one or more undertakings.

Articles 30 to 35 deal with the prohibition or abolition of quantitative restrictions on imports and exports. **Article 36** makes an exception and allows restrictions for a number of reasons including the need to protect industrial and commercial property. The kinds of restrictions involved affect the right of the property owner to specify particular suppliers or trade outlets.

If the Commission believes that it has found a defaulter (which can be a country as well as a

person) it will use any of these Articles or any
others which appear to fit the case. Since the
main goals of the Treaty are eliminating
restrictions and ensuring free competition,
exceptions are not allowed even in cases of
innocent or accidental infringement. Tolerated
breaches of EEC law could create powerful
precedents and lead only to confusion. The
attitude of the Commission is that "interpretation
of the Treaty is a seamless web to prevent
avoidance" as stated in the **Continental Can**
case(2).

Over the years there has developed a large and
complex case law concerning competition in all its
aspects. The account which follows will
concentrate on the law most relevant to
intellectual property, including a few cases for
illustration.

Essentially intellectual property rights can be
exercised, but only their "proper function" will
be tolerated. All other rights will be exhausted
and cease to exist when functions other than the
proper ones are in existence. This means that
rights owners will not be able to exercise certain
aspects of national law in circumstances where the
result would be deemed not to be a legitimate one.

The proper function does not include assertion of
internal boundaries for the purpose of blocking
competition. This was established by **Grundig and
Consten v Commission** in 1966 (3). The manufacturer
Grundig appointed Consten as its exclusive
distributor in France. All its goods had the name
"Grundig" as a trade mark. Consten was assigned
sole use of a second trade mark "GINT". All
primary distributors in other countries were
forbidden to export and any secondary importers
could be stopped by an action for infringement of
the GINT trade mark. The Commission declared that
it was enough, when a brand was as well known as
Grundig, that distributors were prevented from
competing in that brand alone. It was no
justification to plead that distributors could
obtain the same items under different brands.
Therefore Consten was forbidden to sue for
infringement of the GINT mark.

This case illustrates a number of different
points. First, the enterprise has to be large

before it can be a threat to national competitiveness. Secondly, existing national laws cease to operate when they conflict with the aims of the Treaty, and to the extent that they do so. Thirdly, as a general principle, all agreements have to allow for competition from parallel imports (goods which a third party buys in one country and imports into another, usually undercutting the primary distributor in that second country). Competing with such imports ensures that any price differentials are caused only by actual costs which would be incurred also by a parallel importer.

The prime right conferred by industrial property law is that of first putting a protected product on the market. In the case of **Centrafarm v Sterling** 1974, Centrafarm bought a patented drug on the market in Britain, exported it to Holland and sold it there where it was also patented and sold legitimately under the same trade name. As the drug was sold more cheaply in Britain, Centrafarm undercut the Dutch licensee. The Commission held that, once the drug was in circulation in the EEC, the company could not prevent its further purchases and sales. Exactly the same facts and judgment were applied in the case of infringement of the trade mark in **Centrafarm v Winthrop** (4).

However if it is an unauthorised company which first puts the drug on the market then that company can be sued for infringement in the usual way. The authority for this is **Parke, Davis v Probel** 1968 (5).

Rather unfairly, the same attitude as in the Centrafarm cases was twice taken when companies found themselves using the same trade mark accidentally. In **Sirena v Eda** 1971, a US trade mark was assigned to two different owners in Italy and West Germany long before the EEC was thought of (6). The Commission and European Court seemed to be saying that such marks should not be assigned at all as then they no longer indicated the origin of the goods. This is unreasonable as the two markets were quite separate at the time of assignment. In **van Zuylen v Hag** 1974, there were two separate owners of the mark "Hag" in West Germany and in Belgium and Luxembourg because of compulsory sequestration after the Second World

War (7). Here the European Court held that the origins of the split were irrelevant, both marks were legal and had to be allowed to compete. These two are exceptional cases but illustrate the strict no nonsense approach to industrial special pleading taken in the EEC.

Economists often complain that patent monopolies inherently restrict the flow of technology and cannot be justified. However there are provisions for grant of compulsory licences when a market is not being supplied. In the case of **Extrude Hone v Heathway** 1981, a patented invention (machinery and material for abrading or honing surfaces) was manufactured in Ireland for supply to Ireland and the UK. A manufacturer in the UK applied for and was granted a compulsory licence. The ground was that, even though the small market in the UK was being satisfied by imports from Ireland, there was no working of the patent in the UK. The compulsory licence was non-exclusive, so that the importer and the local manufacturer would have to compete (8).

These provisions discussed in terms of trade marks and patents apply just as much to copyright. There have been a number of cases of parallel imports involving gramophone records where rulings to the same effect were made.

Licensing

Patent licences are agreements between undertakings and thus fall under Article 85 of the Treaty of Rome. A regulation was introduced in order to exempt acceptable licences from notification. This regulation lists features of acceptable licence agreements. They must allow parallel imports to exist but a certain amount of exclusivity is permitted, such as an export ban on the licensee, tie-in clauses for the supplies of essential materials and payment of minimum royalties.

It is accepted that licences can increase the number of production facilities and quantity of goods available. It makes it easier for concerns to run the risks of investment. For these reasons grants of exclusive manufacturing rights in all or part of the EEC are permitted automatically, provided they contain safeguards such as those given above.

Automatic clearance prevents a large build up of cases for consideration by the Commission. It also reduces uncertainty. The regulations are complex and rather beyond the scope of this book. One should be aware of their existence and broad aims, for the details of any one case specialist advice is essential(9).

Repackaging of Goods

This is a further way in which the EEC in its robust fashion has allowed the letter of intellectual property law to be relaxed when this is of commercial benefit. Some pharmaceutical companies make money by buying up tablets from another firm and repackaging them. They are redistributed in larger or smaller quantities or in a different format such as in blister packs. Although there is no deception and the original trade mark is replaced, this is unauthorised use of the mark and on a strict interpretation would be forbidden.

The Commission and court have taken the view that repackaging is as good as any other kind of entrepreneurial dealing. No real harm is done and the practice is permitted, provided that repackaging cannot affect the quality of the product, the new wrapping says the product has been repacked and the trade mark holder receives advance notice of marketing the repackaged product.

Summary

This Section has illustrated how the details of cases flesh out and elaborate the principles of the law. It also shows how the influence of the EEC acts to reshape national laws in the interests of international cooperation.

Essentially only the first marketing of goods is allowed. Their subsequent fate is out of the hands of the property owner. Unauthorised first marketing is infringement and can be stopped. Indirect marketing at later stages is now unavoidable competition and has to be tolerated.

Notes and References

References are numbered in sequence for each section separately. A later reference to a work already cited will be referred back. If no section number is given, as in "Ref n above", then the referral is to the same section. Otherwise the entry will read "Ref n, Sect m".
Journal names are extensively abbreviated. For full details please refer to the list below.

Bibliographic Abbreviations

Law Reports

CMLR Common Market Law Reports
FSR Fleet Street Reports
IPD Intellectual Property Decisions
QdR Queensland Law Reports
RPC Reports of Patent, Trade Mark and Design
      Cases

Nearly all legal citations are to the RPC series. Many cases appear in other series as well, but it was thought best to avoid a multiplicity of sources.

Journals

CIPA   Journal of the Chartered Institute of
          Patent Agents, London
CL+P   Computer Law and Practice, Frank Cass,
          London
EIPR   European Intellectual Property Review,
          ESC, Oxford
IIC   International Review of Industrial
          Property and Copyright Law, Max Planck
          Institute for IP Law, Munich. English
          Ed.

J Chem Inf Comput Sci
    Journal of Chemical Information and
    Computer Science, American Chemical
    Society
J Doc   Journal of Documentation, Aslib, London
J Inf Sci   Journal of Information Science
            Institute of Information Scientists,
            London
WPI   World Patent Information, Pergamon,
            Oxford

Research

"MSc Thesis, TCU" and "PhD Thesis, TCU"
refer to theses submitted to the Department of
Information Science at the City University London.
Where possible I refer to papers resulting from
the theses as papers are more accessible.

Bibliography

Section 1 : Industrial Property in General

1. WIPO General Information Booklet, WIPO
    Geneva, 1985.

2. AKR Kiralfy. The English Legal System.
    Sweet+Maxwell, London 7th ed 1984.
    This is a good introduction. There are many
    other books at the same level.

3. Patents Act 1977; 1977 c.37.

4. Registered Designs Act 1949; 12,13 + 14 Geo6
    Ch88.

5. Copyright Act 1956; 4 + 5 Eliz 2. c.74.

6. Department of Trade and Industry.
    Intellectual Property and Innovation
    Cmnd 9712, HMSO London 1986.

7. Trade Mark Act 1938; 1+2 Geo.6. Ch22.

8. TA Blanco White, R Jacob and JD Davies.
    Patents, Trade Marks, Copyright and
    Industrial Designs, 2nd ed. Sweet+Maxwell,
    London 1978.

9. WIPO, Ref 1 above.

10. V Korah. EEC Competition Law and Practice,
    3rd ed. ESC Oxford 1986. This is a very basic
    introduction, Chapter 8 is on industrial
    property rights.

11. L Shaw The Practical Guide for People with a
    New Idea. Lawrence Shaw, London 1982.

Section 2 : Patents

1. A Whittmann, R Schiffels and M Hill. Patent
    Documentation Sweet+Maxwell, London 1979.

2. Statute of Monopolies 1624; 21 Jac. 1 c.3.

3. J Hewish. Rex vs Arkwright 1785 : A Judgment
    for Patents as Information
    WPI **8**(1) 1986 33–37.

4. Patent Law Amendment Act 1852; 16 Vict. c.5.

5. Patents Act 1977; 1977 c.37.

6. Patent Rules 1982, Rules 16, 18-22.

7. The Patent Office, Dept of Trade and
   Industry, London.
   ICIREPAT Codes and Guidelines.
   Patents as a Source of Information.
   How to Prepare a UK Patent Application.

8. J Pinhey, MSc Thesis, TCU 1983, Comparison of
   Patent Family Members.

9. RP Hickman and MJ Roos Workmate CIPA 11(10)
   1982 426-457.

10. Board of Trade. Chairman MAL Banks, The
    British Patent System, Cmnd 4407, HMSO London
    1970.

11. Monsanto Company's (Brignac's) Application
    (1971) RPC 127.

12. Van de Lely v Bamfords (1963) RPC 61.

13. Fomento v Mentmore (1956) RPC 87.

14. Patent Rules 1982, Rule 5.

15. Valensi v British Radio Corporation
    (1973) RPC 337.

16. Johns-Manville Corporation's Patent
    (1967) RPC 479.

17. Beecham Group's (Amoxycillin) Application
    (1980) RPC 261.
18. Anglian Water Authorities' Application
    IPD 5111 1983.

19. Wellcome Foundation's (Hitching's)
    Application (1980) RPC 305.

20. Joos v Commissioner of Patents (1973) RPC 59.

21. Schering's Application (1971) RPC 337.

22. Swift's Application (1962) RPC 37.

23. A Wegner The Chakrabarty Decision
    EIPR 2 1980 304-307.
    DG Daus New Life in US Patents
    EIPR 3(7) 1981 194-200.

24. How to Apply for a British Patent, and
    Introducing Patents The Patent Office,
    London.

25. PA 77 s.16.

26. Department of Trade and Industry Annual
    Report of the Comptroller, Patents, 1985.

27. P Turner Abridgments of British Patents- The
    End of an Era WPI 2(2) 1980 73-76.
    A Hawken The Information Content of Patent
    Abstracts and Abrodgments TCU MSc Thesis
    1985.

28. S Adams and TS Eisenschitz Examination Under
    the Patents Act 1977 CIPA 13 1983 70-86.

29. C Oppenheim Recent Changes in Patent Law J
    Doc 34(3) 1978 217-229.

30. C Oppenheim The Information Function of
    Patents EIPR 1(12) 1979 344-349.

31. Banks Committee, see Ref 9 above, para 114.

32. PA 77 s.62(1) and s.69.

33. PA 77 s.55-59.

34. Pfizer v Ministry of Health (1965) RPC 261.

35. The Times 17 February 1984
    The Observer 19 February 1984.

36. How to get a European Patent, EPO Munich.

37. National Law Relating to the EPC, EPO
    Munich.

38. PD Rosenberg Patent Law Fundamentals. Clark
    Boardman 2nd ed. NY 1986.
    M Petry The US Patent and Trademark System is
    Changing for the Better. CIPA 10(5) 1981
    206-216.

39. Patents Throughout the World. Trade Activities Inc, New York.

40. HM Barton Industrial Property Literature : A Directory of Journals. British Library, London 1981.

41. WIPO General Information Booklet, WIPO Geneva 1985.

42. AH Laird Industrial Property in the Third World CIPA 9(6) 1980 276-287.

43. R Boros Revision of the Paris Convention EIPR 6(2) 1984 46-48.

44. D Perrott The PCT in Use EIPR 4(3) 1982 67-72.

45. D Bartels PCT-Advantages for Applicants in the UK, CIPA Oct 1983 3-15.

46. Community Patent Convention 76/76 EEC. Official Journal of the European Communities 19 L17, 26 January 1976.

47. Luxembourg Conference on the Community Patent Council of the European Communities, Luxembourg 1985.

48. C Oppenheim Patent Office Classification The Inventor Part 1 April 1979 287-291; Part 2 July 1980 8-9.

49. UK Classification Schedules. The Patent Office, London. A Bayer Patent Classification and Information Retrieval Services The Indexer 12(3) 1981 117-124.

50. R Arnott British Patent Classification CIPAPart 1 April 1979 287-291; Part 2 June 1979381-386.

51. JP Britton Recent Developments in the British Patent Classification WPI 5(2) 1983 83-90.

52. S deVries and E deBundel The New Fourth Edition of the IPC WPI 6(2) 1984 58-62 ; see also Editorial, WPI same issue.

53. KJ Dood The US Patent Classification IEEE Transactions on Professional Communications **PC22** 1979 95-100.

54. TS Eisenschitz The Student Research Programme into Patent Information at the City University, London WPI **6**(3) 1984 108-114.

55. NM Williamson Problems of Novelty Searching in Patent Offices TCU MSc Thesis 1970.

56. Online Patent Information Entire issue WPI **7**(1/2) 1985.

57. C Oppenheim Ref 48 above.

58. JH Bryant Automated Patent Searching WPI **5**(4)1983 226-229.

59. JH Bryant, J Terepane and A Kiron Study of Automated Text Searching of US Patents WPI **8**(1) 1986 4-7.

60. Budapest Treaty on Microorganisms WIPO Booklet Section 1 Ref 1.

61. D Bannister and C Oppenheim Information About Microorganisms Contained in Patent Specifications J Chem Inf Comput Sci **19** 1979 123-125.

62. A Bayer Ref 49 above.

63. The Network makes itself known through its newsletter, PIN Bulletin published by the British Library. See also MW Hill, Some Recent Developments in Encouraging Use of Patents as Source of Information, WPI **5**(2) 1983 68-73.

64. H Mann and A Hellyer Coverage of UK Patent Specifications by Abstracting Journals WPI **2**(1) 1980 27-28.

65. J Van den Ende and C Oppenheim Coverage of Microbiological Patents J Chem Inf Comput Sci **21** 1981 124-127.
see also TS Eisenschitz Ref 54 above.

66. W Piltch and W Wratschko INPADOC - A
Computerised Patent Documentation System J
Chem Inf Comput Sci **18**(2) 1978 69-75.

67. PJ Terragno The GET Command WPI **6**(2) 1984
69-73.

68. W Pilch INPADOC - Services for the
Establishment of the Legal Status of Patents
WPI **2**(2) 1980 69-72.

69. C Oppenheim The Patent Services of Derwent
Publications Ltd Sci and Technol Libraries
2(2) 1981 23-31.
MD Dixon and C Oppenheim Derwent
Publications' Patent Information Services.
WPI **4**(2) 1982 60-65.

70. C Oppenheim A Microcomputer Program for the
Statistical Analysis of Patent Databases WPI
5(4) 1983 209-212.
HA van Asselt MSc Thesis TCU 1986.

71. Lexis is run in the UK by Butterworths
Telepublishing Ltd 4-5, Bell Yard, London
WC2. The parent company in the US is Mead
Data Central , Ohio, USA.

72. Lawtel (marketing) Ltd, 46 Bedford Row,
London WC1R 4LR.

73. C Oppenheim Information Aspects of Patents in
Patents in Perspective ed J Phillips, ESC
Oxford 1985.

74. F Liebesny, JW Hewish, PS Hunter and M Hannah
The Scientific and Technical Information
Contained in Patent Specifications OSTI
Report 5177, London 1973 and
The Information Scientist 1974 165-177.

75. J Allen and C Oppenheim The Overlap of US and
Canadian Patent Literature with Journal
Literature WPI **1** 1979 77-80.

76. BK Demidovicz and C Oppenheim The Overlap of
Patent and Journal Literature on Animal
Feedstuffs WPI **3** 1981 82-83.

77. Patents as a technological resource OTAF 8th
Report US Department of Commerce 1977 23-27.

78. TS Eisenschitz and CE Thompson Descriptions
of Microorganisms in Patents and Journal
Articles WPI 4 1982 126-130.
D Young Microbiological Discoveries in
Patents and Other Literature MSc Thesis TCU
1982.

79. TS Eisenschitz, AM Lazard and CJ Willey
Patent Groups and their Relationships with
Journal Literature J Inf Sci 12(1)
1986 35-46.

80. C Oppenheim and EA Sutherland Studies on the
Metallurgical Patent Literature J Chem Inf
Comput Sci 18 1978 122-126 ; 126-129.

81. J Stephenson The Use of Patent Information in
Industry WPI 4(4) 1982 164-171.
J Stephenson Training to Use Patents WPI 4(3)
1982 121-125.

82. PJ Taylor Patent Information and Small Firms
in Merseyside Liverpool City Libraries, 1986.

83. AP deJonge Statistical Evaluation of Patent
Applications WPI 4(2) 1982 56-59.
FJ Leloux Recent Patent Publications WPI
6(3) 1984 130-138.

84. Patent and Citation Studies entire issue WPI
5(3) 1983.
M Dixon Statistical Studies of Patents
Literature PhD Thesis TCU 1982.

85. E Hausser The Use of Patent Information for
the Identification of Development Trends WPI
1(2) 1979 73-76.
JR Leidner The Activities of the Swiss Watch
Industry in the Field of Patent Information
and Documentation WPI 2(4) 1980 159-163.

86. H Kronz and H Grevink Patent Statistics as
Indicators of Technological and Commercial
Trends WPI 2(1) 1980 4-12.
H Kronz and H Grevink IPC and NACE
Classification of Patents WPI 2(3) 1980 103-
115.

87. TS Eisenschitz Ref 54 above.

227

88. TS Eisenschitz The Value of Patent Information in Patents in Perspective Ref 73 above.

89. WR Cornish Employees' Inventions- The New UK Law EIPR **1**(1) 1978 4-6.

90. MJ Hoolahan Employees' Inventions- The Practical Implications EIPR **1** 1979 140-142.

91. FK Beier The Significance of the Patent System for Technical, Economic and Social Progress IIC **11** 1980 563-584.

92. Revision of the Paris Convention, Ref 43 above.

93. Dept of Trade and Industry Intellectual Property Rights and Innovation Cmnd 9117 HMSO London 1983.

94. J Hillman and AG Hamlyn The UK Patent Office on Film WPI **8**(1) 1986.

95. W Kingston An Investment Patent EIPR **7** 1981 207-209.

96. H Kronz Patent Protection for Innovations EIPR **5** 1983 178-183 ; 206-210.

Section 3 : Industrial Copyright and Designs

1. Copyright Act 1956; 4+5 Eliz 2, Ch74.

2. J Phillips and R Whale Whale on Copyright 2nd ed, ESC Oxford, Chapter 1.

3. Report of the Committee to Consider the Law on Copyright and Designs, Chairman Mr Justice Whitford, Cmnd 6732 HMSO, London 1977.

4. Reform of the Law relating to Copyright, Designs and Performers' Protection Cmnd 8301, HMSO London 1981.

5. G Davies Private Copying of Sound and Audio-Visual Recordings ESC, Oxford 1984.

6. C Fellner The Future of Legal Protection for Industrial Designs ESC, Oxford 1985.

7.   Copyright (Amendment) Act 1983; 1983 c.42.

8.   Copyright Act 1956 (Amendment) Act 1982; 1982 c.35.

9.   Department of Trade and Industry Intellectual Property and Innovation Cmnd 9712 HMSO, London 1986.

10. LB(Plastics) v Swish Products (1979) RPC 551.

11. Hensher v Restawhile Upholstery (1975) RPC 31.

12. Solar Thompson v Barton (1977) RPC 537.

13. Registered Designs Act 1949; 12, 13 + 14 Geo 6   c.88.

14. Introducing Design Registration and Applying to Register a Design The Patent Office, London.

15. Design Copyright Act 1968; 1968 c.68.

16. S Gratwick UK Design Copyright EIPR 2(8) 1980 243-245.

17. Dorling v Honnor Marine (1964) RPC 160.

18. Amp v Utilux (1972) RPC 103.

19. Hoover PLC v George Hulme Ltd (1982) FSR 565.

20. British Leyland Motor Corp v Armstrong Patent Co Ltd (1986) FSR 221.

21. Ref 6 above, Ch 8.

22. Ref 6 above, Ch 6.

23. A Turner The Law of Trade Secrets Sweet+Maxwell London 1962.

24. W Ploman and L Clark Hamilton Copyright : Intellectual Property in the Information Age Routledge + Kegan Paul London 1980.

25. D Johnston Design Protection The Design Council, London 1978 Chapter 9.

Section 4 : Trade Marks

1. BC Reid A Practical Introduction to Trade Marks Waterlow, London 1984.

2. Trade Mark Act 1938; 1+2 Geo 6, c.22.

3. Trade Marks (Amendment) Act 1984; 1984 c.19.

4. W Kingston The Political Economy of Innovation Martinus Nijhoff 1984.

5. How to Apply for a Registered Trade Mark, The Patent Office, London.

6. C Morcom Character Merchandising EIPR 1 1978 7-10.

7. Holly Hobbie TM (1983) FSR 138.

8. Ref 1 above Ch.9.

9. Lego System Ak v Lego M Lemelstrich Ltd (1983) FSR 155.

10. Bollinger v Costa Brava Wine (1960) RPC 16; (1961) RPC 116.

11. Annabel's v Schock (1972) RPC 838.

12. McCulloch v Lewis May (1947) 65 RPC 58.

13. Wombles v Wombles Skips (1977) RPC 99.

14. R Durie Case Comment EIPR 3(1) 1981 24-27.

15. Cadbury-Schweppes v Pub Squash Co Ltd (1981) RPC 429.

16. European Trade Marks Office - The Race Is On Trademark World June 1986 18-19.

17. Ref 5 above.

18. White Paper Ref 6, Section 1, Para 1.18.

19. C Oppenheim The Patent Office Databases on Pergamon Infoline WPI 8(3) 1986 185-192.

20. D Rossiter A New Dimension in Trademark Searching for the Pharmaceutical Industry Trademark World 1(3) 1986 34-37.

Section 5 : Related Legislation

1. RS Crespi Patenting in the Biological Sciences John Wiley 1983.

2. RS Crespi Biotechnology Patents - A Case of Special Pleading EIPR 7(7) 1985 190-194.

3. Budapest Treaty 1977, WIPO General Information Booklet, WIPO Geneva, Ann ed.

4. D Bannister and C Oppenheim Sect 2 , Ref 61.

5. D MacKenzie Seeds of Conflict over Food Genes New Scientist 22/29 December 1983 870-871.

6. G Dworkin The Plant Varieties Act 1983 EIPR 5(10) 1983 270-275.

7. See Sect 2, 4.1.1 under the definition of an inventor.

8. J Borking Software Potection in Europe CL+P 1 1984 6-9 ; 42-47.

9. DG Jerrard Review of Software Protection CL+P 1(1) 1984 2-5.

10. D Chisum Copyright, Computer Programs and the Apple Cases EIPR 5(9) 1983 233-237.

11. RH Stern Infringement of Copyright when Computer Programs achieve the same Results EIPR 7(5) 1985 123-125.

12. GB 1472056.

13. Copyright (Computer Software) Amendment Act 1985, 1985 c.41.

14. White Paper, Ref Sect 1, no 6, Chapter 9.

15. MS Keplinger and RW Frase, Role of CONTU in Computers and Photocopying. IEEE Transactions on Professional Communications, PC20 1977 167-170.

231

16. Ref 10 above.

17. Whelan v Jaslow Dental Laboratory, Ref 11 above.

18. RH Stern Brief analysis of the Semiconductor
    Chip Protection Act 1984   EIPR 6(10) 1984
    291-294.
    FM Greguras and NM Williams Operational
    Impact of the Semiconductor Chip Protection
    Act CL+P 1(5) 1984 159-164.

19. J Lahore The Apple Computer Case and
    Australian Law EIPR 6(7) 1984 196-203.
    G Hughes Computer Software Copyright   CL+P
    2(6) 1986 174-177.

20. S Elsom Software Protection Practice CL+P
    1985 1(6) 190-192.

21. A Staines The Consumer as Enemy CL+P 2(5)
    1986 138-140.

22. Coco v Clark (1969) RPC 41.
    See also Facienda Chicken Ltd v Fowler
    1986 FSR 291.

23. The Law Commission Breach of Confidence
    Report No 110. Cmnd 8388, HMSO London 1981.
    This contains a good survey of relevant
    cases.

24. J Michael The Politics of Secrecy, Penguin
    Books London 1982.

25. Attorney General v Jonathan Cape Ltd (1976)
    QB 752.

26. Distillers v Times Newspapers (1975) QB 613.

27. Schering Chemicals Ltd v Falkman Ltd (1981) 2
    WLR 848.

28. A Coleman Case Comment EIPR 7(8) 1985
    234 - 235.

29. P Heims Countering Industrial Espionage 20th
    Century Security, Leatherhead 1982.

30. TS Eisenschitz Theft of Trade Secrets EIPR
    6(4) 1984 91-92; 6(9) 1984 266.

31. A Coleman Breach of Confidence EIPR 3 1982 73-78. See also Ref 23 above.

32. Franklin v Giddins (1978) QdR 72.

33. A Crook Data Protection in the UK J Inf Sci 7 1983 15-22; 47-57.

34. Data Protection Act 1984; 1984 c.35.

35. R Rowell Counterfeiting and Forgery: A Practical Guide to the Law, Butterworths, London 1986.

36. TA Blanco White et al. Ref 8, Sect 1 108-111.

Section 6 : EEC Competition Law

1. B Rudden and D Wyatt, Eds, Basic Community Laws Clarendon Press Oxford 1980.

2. Europemballage Corp and Continental Can Co Inc v Commission (1973) CMLR 199.

3. Consten and Grundig v EEC Commission 1966 CMLR 418.

4. Centrafarm v Sterling Drug (1974) 2 CMLR 480 Centrafarm v Winthrop (1974) 2 CMLR 480.

5. Parke, Davis & Co v Probel (1968) CMLR 47.

6. Sirena v Eda (1971) CMLR 260.

7. van Zuylen Freres v Hag (1974) 2 CMLR 127.

8. Extrude Hone Corp v Heathway Ltd (1981) 32 CMLR 379.

9. V Korah EEC Competition Law and Practice 3rd Ed ESC Oxford 1986 Ch.8.

INDEX